To
Danny Cipriani, Thérèse & Gerard Bennett,
Ann-Marie Rooney, Ronan O'Gara,
Fran LaMude, Phyllis Martin, Majella Ledwith,
Mary Fagan, all at LARCC and Abbey Blooms,
Kath O'Grady Reilly, Brendan & Debbie Monaghan,
Margaret & Matt Lennon, Cieran & Teresa Temple,
John O'Grady

"We read to know we are not alone"
(C. S. Lewis in the film 'Shadowlands')

"The answers are all out there, we just need to ask the right questions."
(Oscar Wilde)

"We are all held in God's love.
What we lack is awareness."

Contents

Introduction

The Doors were an American rock band formed in Los Angeles in 1965 with vocalist Jim Morrison, keyboard Ray Manzarek, guitarist Robby Krieger and drummer John Densmore. Jim Morrison was the charismatic frontman and writer. His last great vocal was "Riders on the Storm". It begins:

> Riders on the storm
> Riders on the storm
> Into this house, we're born
> Into this world, we're thrown
> Like a dog without a bone
> An actor out on loan
> Riders on the storm
>
> There's a killer on the road
> His brain is squirmin' like a toad
> Take a long holiday
> Let your children play
> If you give this man a ride
> Sweet family will die
> Killer on the road, yeah
>
> Girl, you gotta love your man
> Girl, you gotta love your man
> Take him by the hand
> Make him understand
> The world on you depends
> Our life will never end
> Gotta love your man, yeah
>
> Riders on the storm
> Riders on the storm

There was a Country and Western song called "Ghost Riders in the Sky". Jim Morrison changed this to "Riders on the Storm" in his song. In his college years Morrison would hitch-hike many miles to see his girlfriend. He began to think of himself as a wandering rider on the storm. The hitchhiker was a powerful symbol form Morrison who saw himself as exploring new ways. It speaks to a sense of transience. Morrison's hitchhiker becomes a killer. This was based on a real-life serial killer Billy Cook who haunted Morrison's memory. Between 1950 and 1951 Billy Cook murdered five people as he hitchhiked. Ray Manzarek's keyboard creates a sinister atmosphere echoed by Robby Krieger's guitar. Manzarek's solo in the middle seems to echo the sound of falling rain. Morrison's vocals add to the feeling of unease in the song.

When Morrison was a student in UCLA he took a course by Jack Hirschman on philosophy. He read Camus, Sartre and Nietzsche. He also came across Martin Heidegger (+1976) whose work "Being and Time"[1] speaks about the way we are "thrown into the world". We find ourselves in the world without having asked to be here. We are confronted by the questions: who am I? Where do I belong? Morrison uses this in his song. This speaks to our finding ourselves in the world.

In the world of the Old Testament, the Book of Ecclesiastes wrestles with these questions. Morrison had called on the girl he loved to hold his hand so he wouldn't be lost. Qoheleth, the preacher in Ecclesiastes, finds life to be meaningless. He uses the Hebrew word 'hebel' which means something that vanishes like the early mist in the morning. Hebel means "vapour" or breath literally. Qoheleth finds himself thrown into a world he cannot understand. His voice stands for those who find life confusing and meaningless.

In this book I wrestle with Qoheleth and his pessimism. In the world of the Old Testament there are many voices, as if they were debating with each other. Walter Brueggemann uses the metaphor of a court-drama[2] to account for all the different voices. Qoheleth is one such voice. He brings home to us that we are "thrown into this world" and he struggled to find meaning. This prods us to wrestle with his words and see can we answer him. We are "riders on the storm" and we seek to find out who we are and do we matter. This is the heart of the book.

[1] Martin Heidegger, Being and Time (New York: 2010, originally published 1927).

[2] Walter Brueggemann, Theology of the Old Testament (Minneapolis: 2005).

Chapter One

The Invisibles

In 2020 the journalist Victoria Derbyshire met a young woman named Daisy who was sleeping rough in London. The worst thing about rough sleeping was not the cold nights or the discomfort of a makeshift bed. Rather "the worst thing about rough sleeping is not being seen" (BBC 2020). This is a view many have discovered. Mark Horvath is the founder of the 'Invisible People' project. He tells the story of a homeless man living in Los Angeles. He said:

> "For years, the man assumed he was invisible because no one would look at him. That is until a boy handed him a pamphlet one day and the man responded, 'What! You can see me? How can you see me? I'm invisible!' "[1]

We can have an impact on others by directing, or failing to direct, our gaze. By fixing our attention on someone is a way of acknowledging others' existence. By turning away our gaze we can make the person feel like a nobody. There are many such people in homes and hospitals who are ill who never receive any visitors. They feel lost and alone. There are many who are abused and are not listened to. I have heard medical people say to an abused person, "You must get over it." Without help or acceptance this is impossible. The world becomes lonelier still. In the case of the homeless we might avoid 'seeing' them because we live in a society that enables their predicament and there is a feeling of hopelessness and helplessness in the face of this society. Their plight can remind us that our lives are comfortable while theirs are not.

---

[1] as quoted in Silvia Caprioglio Panizza, The Ethics of Attention: Enjoying the Real with Iris Murdoch and Simone Weil (London: 2022), p. 1. For more on this sort of experience see E. Kramer and E. Hsieh, Gaze as Embodied Ethics: Homelessness, the Other, and Humanity in M. Dutta and D. Zapata (eds.), Communicating for Social Change: Meaning, Power and Resistance (Singapore: 2019), p. 33-62.

Simone Weil (+1943) was a French philosopher, mystic and political activist. She was the younger of two children. Her older brother, André, (+1998) was a famous mathematician. She had a close relationship with him. He did important work in number theory and algebraic geometry. He was a founding member of the Bourbaki group. This was a pseudonym under which his group published.

However, when Simone was young she suffered in the shadow of her brother. She was depressed when she was not able to be the same intellectual genius as her brother André was already becoming at an early age. She put it this way:

> "At fourteen I fell into one of those pits of bottomless despair which come with adolescence, and I seriously thought of dying because of the mediocrity of my natural faculties. The exceptional gifts of my brother, who had a childhood and youth comparable to those of Pascal, brought my own inferiority home to me. I did not mind having no visible successes, but what did grieve me was the idea of being excluded from that transcendent kingdom to which only the truly great have access and wherein truth abides. I preferred to die rather than live without that truth. After months of inward darkness, I suddenly had the everlasting conviction that any human being, even though practically devoid of natural faculties, can penetrate to the kingdom of truth reserved for genius, if only he longs for truth and perpetually concentrates all his attention upon its attainment."[2]

This was her first "conversion" and led her to become a student of philosophy. She emphasised the importance of attentiveness to the other and with others. She explained these in her essays for her teacher, Emile Chartier (also known as Alain).

After she qualified she took various jobs such as writing, teaching and being a political activist. She worked in workers' education classes. To

[2] see Simone Weil, Spiritual Autobiography, in Waiting on God (London: 1942), p. 18-49.

get first hand experience of the plight of workers she obtained employment in a factory in 1934 and later she got a job working for Renault. The work appalled her – the way it destroyed the spirit of both herself and her fellow workers, making them unable to think or choose, by numbing them and reducing them to senseless things, little better than the machines they worked. The feelings this induced in her she gave the name "affliction". She describes it thus:

> "Affliction makes God appear to be absent for a time, more absent than a dead man, more absent than light in the utter darkness of a cell. A kind of horror submerges the whole soul. During this absence there is nothing to love. What is terrible is that if, in this darkness, there is nothing to love, the soul ceases to love, God's absence becomes final."[3]

Putting all these different pictures together we see how people are dehumanised. Those who live on the streets are invisible. Many have mental illnesses but they find no comfort. Those who work in employment that dehumanises them are invisible and feel dispirited. Simone Weil spoke of this and how after she left work she felt less than human and was nervous even getting on public transport. We live in a lonely world. So many people feel worthless and unloved. It is the disease of our times. Simone Weil explored this feeling and sought to understand this feeling. She did not spare herself in her quest for truth. For this seeking she used the word "attention" (in French "attente") meaning we invest ourselves in getting to know the truth. It is also an important word for inter-personal relationships – we give the other person the fullness of our attention to show we are invested in them. It also has the connotations of 'waiting' for the truth to show itself.

Healing Affliction:

Simone's family were nominally Jewish. In fact they didn't practice at all. Simone considered herself at an early age to be an agnostic. She was

---

[3] Simone Weil, Waiting for God, p. 80.

passionately interested in giving people their dignity and would give herself to this cause. She opposed fascism and nihilism. She volunteered to fight in the Spanish Civil War on the Republican side. She was put on machine gun duty but she was quickly removed from this duty. She was as great a danger to her own side as she was to the enemy. She had been a pacifist after she left University but she saw in Germany the rise of Hitler and his violence. This initially made her abandon her pacifism but in the Civil War she saw how force and its use dehumanises us. She abandoned the Spanish Civil War eventually. She experienced "affliction" again. Life was difficult for her. In the factions she saw how people were dehumanised and just cogs in the machine. In Fascism she saw how people were dehumanised again. In War she saw how people were liquidated. Her health was fragile and she suffered violent headaches. The word "affliction" is the translation of the French word 'malheur' which doesn't have an exact English translation. 'Affliction' is the usual word we use. 'Affliction' ('Malheur') can destroy us as persons. André Gide called her "the patron saint of outsiders".

All of this 'Malheur', where she felt her life had been drained from her, was a preparation for her meeting with God. She felt she wasn't the one who sought God but it was he who sought her. Her philosophical hero was Plato. He spoke about an ideal world where the perfect lives and our world is just a reflection of this ideal world. She spoke of how in a moment of intense suffering where she was forcing herself to feel love she sensed a personal, loving presence. She didn't want to name this love. She didn't know what was to come, but she was certain of that presence and this presence was real, more real than the presence of any human being.

She was prepared for this experience by other experiences in her life. After her experiences of the unbearable working and living conditions, which so many people have no choice but to endure, were exacerbated by her violent migraines, she was emotionally exhausted and in wretched physical condition. Her parents brought her to Portugal in 1934 to give her a holiday. In a tiny fishing village she witnessed a procession in honour of the local patron saint. She saw the women...

"making a tour of all the ships, carrying candles and singing what must have been very ancient hymns of a heart-rending sadness."

(Waiting for God, p. 26)

The experience was beyond words. She felt the passion and praise in the prayers. She felt the women's pain. Suddenly she writes

"the conviction was borne in upon me that Christianity is pre-eminently the religion of slaves, that slaves cannot help belonging to it, and I among others."

(Waiting for God, p. 26)

The second of her three mystical experiences came in 1934 when she visited the chapel of Santa Maria degli Angeli "where St. Francis often used to pray" (Waiting for God, p. 26). There she described an event in which "something stronger than her ... compelled her for the first time in her life to go down on her knees" (p. 26). She knelt, not out of any selfish desire or fulfillment of a ritual obligation. It was her response to an experience of love. The last of her experiences occurred when she was at the Benedictine Abbey of Solesmes in 1938. She was suffering again from her headaches. She heard the monks singing the Gregorian chants and she was filled with "a pure and perfect joy" (p. 26). This provided a great relief from her suffering and showed her the possibility "of loving divine love in the midst of affliction" (p. 26). She was introduced to George Herbert's poem "Love" by an English Catholic. She memorised this poem and would often recite it.

"at the culminating point of a violent headache....It was during one of these recitations that...Christ himself came down and took possession of [her]."

(Waiting for God, p. 27)

Herbert's poem reads as follows:

LOVE bade me welcome; yet my soul drew back,
    Guilty of dust and sin.

But quick-eyed Love, observing me grow slack
    From my first entrance in,
Drew nearer to me, sweetly questioning
    If I lack'd anything.

'A guest,' I answer'd, 'worthy to be here':
    Love said, 'You shall be he.'
'I, the unkind, ungrateful? Ah, my dear,
    I cannot look on Thee.'
Love took my hand, and smiling did reply,
    'Who made the eyes but I?'

'Truth, Lord; but I have marr'd them: let my shame
    Go where it doth deserve.'
'And know you not,' says Love, 'who bore the blame?'
    'My dear, then I will serve.'
'You must sit down,' says Love, 'and taste my meat.'
    So I did sit and eat.

For her these experiences were not the opposite of philosophy, but the consequence of philosophical analytics. Philosophy can bring us to a state where we are more open to these experiences. Now Weil felt in the middle of her suffering "the presence of a love, like that which one can read in the smile of a beloved face" (Waiting for God, p. 27). She had experienced the presence and healing power of love in Jesus. It was this that convinced her he was the incarnation of God's love. She knew from experience (Waiting for God, p. 28). Weil believed this was the way for people to come to know God in Jesus. They would come to him by experience not by ideas but by encounter with the living God. Her writings would be collected and gathered together after she died. She published comparatively little in her lifetime. Her writings would influence people like Pope John XXIII, Paul VI, Albert Camus and Iris Murdoch. Simone Weil felt that our meeting with God was similar to two people arranging to meet but cannot find each other. They are both present but cannot see each other.

After her experiences she had to leave France because of the Nazi invasion. Even though she and her family were non-practising Jews this would mean nothing to the Nazis. She emigrated to America and eventually found herself in England. She died there in 1943. She refused to eat properly, insisting on eating only the rations the people in France lived on. She did not join the Catholic Church even though some claim she was baptised but there is no proof of this as yet.[4]

Simone wrote that "the beauty of this world is Christ's tender smile coming to us through matter" (Waiting for God, p. 164-165). She also said that "beauty captivates the flesh in order to obtain permission to pass right to the soul" (p. 165). She spoke of attention consisting of suspending or emptying one's thought such that one is ready to receive (or be penetrated by) the object to which one turns one's gaze, be that object one's neighbour or ultimately, God (Waiting for God, p111ff). Attention is the very substance of prayer. When one prays, one empties oneself and fixes one's gaze on God and becomes ready to receive God (Waiting for God, p. 105). Similarly we can love people by emptying ourselves and receiving our neighbour is all of his or her truth, asking our neighbour: "What are you going through?" (Waiting for God, p. 114ff).

While she was in London she met De Gaulle, the leader of the Free French. She asked to be parachuted behind enemy lines and she could work for the Resistance. De Gaulle said she was unable to hold a rifle, was ill and had difficulty with sight. He said she was "crazy". Yet there is now evidence that Weil was recruited by the Special Operations Executive, with a view to sending her back to France as a clandestine radio operator. However, her health was failing at this time.[5] Richard Rees sums up her dying and death in the following words: "As for her death, whatever explanation one may give of it will amount in the end to saying that she died of love."[6]

---

[4] After her death stories started to circulate that Simone had been baptised by her friend Simone Deitz, on her deathbed.
see Eric O. Springsted, The Baptism of Simone Weil, in Spirit, Nature and Community: Issues in the Thought of Simone Weil, Diogenes Allen and Eric O. Springsted (eds.), (Albany, N.Y.: 1994), p. 3-18.
[5] Simone Weil by Nigel Perrin, Archived 2012-12-10 at Archive Today.
[6] Richard Rees, Simone Weil: A Sketch for a Portrait (Oxford: 1966), p. 191.

The Believer of the Future:

At critical times in history when all seemed lost, God rose up mystics who were lights in the darkness. Julian of Norwich appeared during the Black Death. Simone appeared during World War II. Her words became better known after the war in the "age of anxiety". Karl Rahner (+1984) famously said "the devout Christian of the future will either be a 'mystic', one who has experienced 'something', or he will cease to be anything at all."[7] Rahner was a German Jesuit priest and theologian who deeply influenced Catholic thought and Christian thought generally.

His point of departure for his thought is God's self-communication to the human person. Our dignity is to be the one addressed and called. He believes that all people receive God, though in a hidden way. God is not a being among others but is the incomprehensible ground of being. He is a personal, loving mystery whom we can address as "Thou". God is Love (1 Jn 4:8,16).

The experience of grace is the experience of mysticism. It grounds the ordinary experience of faith, life and love and it is the basis of one acting according to one's conscience. Within each of us is a longing for peace, love and happiness. This is an experience of grace. This longing for love contains a primordial experience of God. We find God's presence in our daily experience of life. We are carried along as we find meaning in our lives. In the end that goal is "God himself towards whose second coming, in the person of Christ, our future moves inexorably."[8] We all see what we want from life and what we actually receive. There is a profound emptiness in our hearts.

The hunger of the heart is revealed in the mistaken belief that someone or something will fulfill us totally. To be human is an immense longing. As a child we want one toy; as a young man to belong to the right group, to get into the right school, or date the right person; as an adult to obtain

---

[7] Karl Rahner, Christian Living Formerly and Today, Theological Investigations, VII, p. 15. see also Karl Rahner, Rahner in Dialogue, Conversation and Interviews, 1965-1982 (New York: 1986), p. 15.

[8] Karl Rahner, Belief Today (New York: 1967), p. 20f.

the right position, find the right note, and the like. Yet when we obtain our heart's desire, we soon discover it is never enough. The heart is a lonely hunter and it does not rest until it rests in God. The immense longing we feel is nothing less than a desire to rest in God and his love. Rahner said in an interview:

> "Is human existence absurd or does it have ultimate meaning? If it is absurd, why do human beings have an unquenchable hunger for meaning? Is it not a consequence of God's existence? For if God doesn't exist, then the hunger for meaning is absurd."[9]

This is actually our experience of God who dwells in the heart of our being. It is from this hidden presence that we experience life. This 'emptiness' is a call from God to come to know him. All the good things we experience in our daily lives are intimations of the divine. God is in us and with us.

In the Gospels we find Jesus at wedding feasts, at banquets, changing water into wine and making food available for the hungry. Our happiness was and is his concern. He shares our joys as well as our sorrows. Rahner goes on to discuss the ways God is present. He says:

> "Let me repeat, though I may say it in almost the same words: where the one and entire hope is given beyond all individual hopes, which comprehends all impulses in silent promise,
> - where a responsibility in freedom is still accepted and borne where it has no apparent offer of success and advantage,
> - where a man experiences and accepts his ultimate freedom which no earthly compulsions can take away from him,
> - where the leap into the darkness of death is accepted as the beginning of everlasting promise,

---

[9] Karl Rahner, Faith in a Wintry Season (New York: 1989), p. 163.

- where the sum of all accounts of life, which no one can calculate alone, is understood by the incomprehensible Other as good, though it still cannot be 'proven',
- where the fragmentary experience of love, beauty, and joy is experienced and accepted purely and simply as the promise of love, beauty, and joy, without their being understood in ultimate cynical skepticism as a cheap form of consolation for some final deception,
- where the bitter, deceptive, and vanishing everyday world is withstood until the accepted end and accepted out of a force whose ultimate source is still unknown to us but can be tapped by us,
- where one dares to pray into a silent darkness and knows that one is heard, although no answer seems to come back about which one might argue and rationalize,
- where one lets oneself go unconditionally and experiences this capitulation as true victory,
- where falling becomes true uprightness
- where desperation is accepted and is still secretly accepted as trustworthy without cheap trust
- where a man entrusts all his knowledge and all his questions to the silent and all-inclusive mystery which is loved more than all our individual knowledge which makes us such small people
- where we rehearse our own death in everyday life and try to live in such a way as we would like to die, peaceful and composed[10]

Rahner sees God's Holy Spirit at work in all the circumstances of our life. He wants us to see the work of Spirit in the people we meet, the joys and sorrows we experience. God is always close to us. In all those events we experience true hope and our life rests in God. Rahner was known as the mystic of everyday life. True beauty is when we see all things with the eyes of love. We live in the hope that in the end we will

---

[10] Karl Rahner, Reflections on the Problem of the Gradual Ascent to Christian Perfection, Theological Investigations, XIX, p. 147.

find peace. In the Book of Revelation we read: "He will dwell with them, and they shall be his people, and God himself will be with them; he will wipe away every tear from their eyes, and death shall be no more, neither shall there be mourning nor crying nor pain any more, for the former things have passed away" (Rev 21: 3-4). Seeing God in all things prepares us for this new Heaven and the new Earth.

"If Music be the Food of Love, Play On"
(Shakespeare, Twelfth Night):

Others found God in music. The works of Mozart were important for people such as Karl Barth, Hans Urs Von Balthasar, Soren Kierkegaard and Pope Benedict XIV. Karl Barth wrote:

> "Wolfgang Amadeus Mozart. Why is it that this man is so incomparable? Why is it that for the receptive, he has produced in almost every bar he conceived and composed a type of music for which "beautiful" is not a fitting epithet: music which for the true Christian is not mere entertainment, enjoyment or edification but food and drink; music full of comfort and counsel for his needs; music which is never a slave to its technique nor sentimental but always "moving," free and liberating because wise, strong and sovereign? Why is it possible to hold that Mozart has a place in theology, especially in the doctrine of creation and also in eschatology, although he was not a father of the Church, does not seem to have been a particularly active Christian, and was a Roman Catholic, apparently leading what might appear to us a rather frivolous existence when not occupied in his work? It is possible to give him this position because he knew something about creation in its total goodness that neither the real fathers of the Church nor our Reformers, neither the orthodox nor Liberals, neither the exponents of natural theology nor those heavily armed with the "Word of God," and certainly not the Existentialists, nor indeed any other great musicians before

and after him, either know or can express and maintain as he did. In this respect he was pure in heart, far transcending both optimists and pessimists."[11]

Mozart wrote at the time of the Lisbon Earthquake. This took place in 1755 in the Iberian Peninsula and Northwest Africa. Estimates vary as to the number of people who died in Lisbon, but there were many thousands. There was an air of sadness around Europe and a tone of despair. Mozart's music celebrates life in the face of despair. There is an affirmation of life in his music. This is what Barth experienced when he listened to Mozart. In the face of chaos Mozart produces a harmony and his music points to a peace that passes our understanding. He sees creation and music as praising our creator.

> "I make this interposition here, before turning to chaos, because in the music of Mozart – and I wonder whether the same can be said of any other works before or after – we have clear and convincing proof that it is a slander on creation to charge it with a share in chaos because it includes a Yes and a No, as though orientated to God on the one side and nothingness on the other. Mozart causes us to hear that even on the latter side, and therefore in its totality, creation praises its Master and is therefore perfect. Here on the threshold of our problem – and it is no small achievement – Mozart has created order for those who have ears to hear, and he has done it better than any scientific deduction could."
>
> (Church Dogmatics, III/3, p. 299)

Grief and tragedy are not the end. We see this in Jesus who underwent the pain of Good Friday to come to the day of Resurrection. Mozart's music, for Barth, pointed to the final victory of God when "every tear will be wiped away" (Rev 21:4). He experienced God's beauty and presence in Mozart's music.

---

[11] Karl Barth, Church Dogmatics III/3, (Edinburgh: 2004), p. 297f.

Many people have experienced happiness and release in listening to their favourite music. It can bring peace to a troubled soul. This is an intuition of the peace we hope to find in God.

Another Outsider:

Through the different people we have looked at we see there are people who have to find God in their lives. Simone Weil experienced Christ's love. Rahner sees God in the ordinary. Karl Barth found God in the word of God, but at the same time the beauty of Mozart's music helped him praise God. In my own life I have met people who were with me when I was very ill and not expected to live. Some knew mystically that I was in bad shape and they prayed with love for my healing.

At this stage the reader can ask, What about me: Can I find God? There is no road guide for this. The truth is it is God who seeks us first. The encounter of each person with God is unique to that person. We can, however, prepare for an encounter. Simone Weil said that if we find God we need solitude and silence. Many can be afraid of this silence because we encounter things in ourselves we do not like. Yet if we can enter the silence we are held in the loving grasp of God. He reveals his love in Jesus. When Simone prayed she experienced his love in her heart. We can do the same.

To add to this we can meditate on scripture and meet God in his word. This was the project Karl Barth went on in his life – beginning with Paul's Letter to the Romans.

Simone Weil spoke of our meeting with God in the following words:

> "God and humanity are like two lovers who have missed their rendezvous. Each is there before the time, but each at a different place, and they wait, and wait, and wait. He stands motionless, nailed to the spot for the whole of time. She is distraught and impatient. But alas for her if she gets tired and goes away. ...The crucifixion of Christ is the

image of the fixity of God. God is attention without distraction. One must imitate the patience and humility of God."[12]

Even if we think we have missed God, he is still there seeking us. We have to wait with attention, in hope.

I take the book of Ecclesiastes as our meeting place. It is not like any other book of the Old Testament. It begins by claiming that the words are "the words of the Teacher, the son of David, king in Jerusalem" (Ecc 1:1). The lateness of the Hebrew language used shows us that the work is later. It was a common fiction to attribute works of wisdom to Solomon, the son of David. The teacher translates the Hebrew name Qoheleth. His name means preacher, assembler or gatherer. The NRSV translates his name as teacher. Luther translated the name as preacher.

In the next line we begin to see why Qoheleth is different. He says

"Vanity of vanities, says the Teacher;
Vanity of vanities! All is vanity."

(Ecc 1:2 NRSV)

Vanity translates the Hebrew word '*hebel*'. This is another form of the name 'Abel' who was murdered by his brother Cain (see Genesis 4:1-18). The word '*hebel*' means a mist or vapour that disappears. Everything, according to Qoheleth, is empty and meaningless. Everything is empty, a great emptiness. This theme runs throughout Ecclesiastes.

In Herman Melville's 'Moby Dick' is a story of a chase after evil which is evil and futile, and destructive. Melville recognises the truth of 'Vanity of vanities' (Moby Dick, chap. 96). Twentieth-century literature reflects the meaninglessness many people find in life. We see the despair and hollowness of Willy Loman in Arthur Miller's 'Death of a

---

[12] Simone Weil, The Things of the World, in G. A. Panichas (ed.) The Simone Weil Reader (Philadelphia: 1979), p. 424f.

Salesman', the blurring of truth and falsehood in George Orwell's '1984' and the plight of T.S. Eliot's 'Hollow Man'. Qoheleth goes on to say: "Therefore I hated life because the work that was done under the sun was distressing to me, for all is vanity and chasing of the wind." (Ecc 2:17). Why is this work in the Canon, the books of Scripture? When we read it aloud we see it is 'the word of God'. Qoheleth gives a voice to those who feel that they hate life. The 'vanity of vanities' speaks to the heart of those who feel invisible and don't matter. it gives a voice to people like 'Daisy' who we met at the start of this chapter. This voice is placed before God and all the people who feel the 'vanity of vanities' find a voice.

At the end of the Book the editor says: "The words of the wise are like goads, their collected sayings like finely embedded nails..." (Ecc 12:11). Qoheleth is like an early Kierkegaard. Kierkegaard's nickname was the "fork" – this came to be understood as the way his words and books make us think and come to know ourselves. Qoheleth, in his own way and time, does the same.

Psalm 39 helps us see the journey we are on. this psalm was used by Igor Stravinsky in his 1930 work "Symphony of Psalms". The first part of the psalm is Qoheleth-like:

> I said, "I will watch my ways
>   and keep my tongue from sin;
> I will put a muzzle on my mouth
>   while in the presence of the wicked."
> So I remained utterly silent,
>   not even saying anything good.
> But my anguish increased;
> my heart grew hot within me.
> While I meditated, the fire burned;
>   then I spoke with my tongue:
> "Show me, Lord, my life's end
>   and the number of my days;
>   let me know how fleeting my life is.
> You have made my days a mere handbreadth;

the span of my years is as nothing before you.
Everyone is but a breath,
    even those who seem secure.[b]
"Surely everyone goes around like a mere phantom;
    in vain they rush about, heaping up wealth
    without knowing whose it will finally be.

(Ps 39:1-6)

Ps 39 articulates despair and hope. The opening lines show the difficulties of life. The psalmist found it hard to speak but he does articulate his feelings in prayer. This is done before God in whom he places his trust. The pain he was in brought him sorrow and inner turmoil.

"Hear my prayer, Lord,
    listen to my cry for help;
    do not be deaf to my weeping.
I dwell with you as a foreigner,
    a stranger, as all my ancestors were.
  Look away from me, that I may enjoy life again
    before I depart and am no more."

(Ps 39:12-13)

He has faith that God will hear his voice and soothe his tears. His words show us that our true home is in God himself. In the face of his despair he hopes in God and has faith that his prayer is heard. This psalm helps us see how to pray Qoheleth. We can feel 'The Vanity of Vanities' but we can wait in hope for God to hear our distress and soothe our tears. We have, to use Simone Weil's words, to wait with attention, in faith and hope. John of the Cross spoke of the 'Dark Night of the Soul' but the dark night gives way to new life in the Spirit.

Chapter 2

The Silence of God

When Jesus was nailed to the cross – and hung there in torment - he cried out – "God, my God! Why hast thou forsaken me?" He cried out as loud as he could. He thought that his heavenly father had abandoned him. He believed everything he'd ever preached was a lie. The moments before he died, Christ was seized by doubt. Surely that must have been his greatest hardship? God's silence.

– Ingmar Bergman

This is a scene from 'Winter Light' when the pastor Tomas is wrestling with doubt and the feeling of failure. This formed part of Bergman's trilogy. The first part of the trilogy was 'Through a Glass Darkly' (1961) where the silence of God is implied. In 'Winter Light' the silence of God is referred to directly (1962) and the trilogy finishes with a film called 'The Silence'. 'The Silence' focusses on two sisters, the younger a sensuous woman with a young son, the elder sister is more intellectually orientated and seriously ill. It examines their tense relationship as they travel through central Europe. Bergman pointed out there is no theology is it, only the lack of it. Qoheleth wrestled with the silence of God: "God is in heaven and you are on earth, so let your words be few" (Ecc 5:2).

Rollo May uses the term schizoid to mean out of touch, avoiding close relationships, the inability to feel.[1] He uses the term as the general condition of our world and culture and the tendencies of people who make it up. Many significant dramatists are those who take the subject matter of this inability to communicate, this avoiding relationships. In this group belongs such people as Ionesco, Genet, Beckett and Pinter. In painting Paul Cézanne painted this broken, schizoid world. He put down on canvas in his landscapes the struggle he felt inside. He shows the

---

[1] Rollo May, Love and Will (New York: 2007), p, 16.

landscapes from different points of view at the one time, making it difficult for us to see where we are. In this he directly inspired the Cubists such as Picasso and Braque. They see the world differently. He was sensitive to the underlying psychic conflicts in himself and in our world and could present the broken world as it is in its deepest form. Picasso said "We love Cézanne because of his anxiety." In looking at a Cézanne landscape is a healing effect. We are put in touch with our inner brokenness. Acceptance of who and what we are is the beginning of a healing journey. I call Qoheleth the Cézanne of the Bible. He shows the broken nature of reality and puts words on that experience. We can call out with the psalmist...

> But as for me, I am poor and needy;
>   may the Lord think of me.
> You are my help and my deliverer;
>   you are my God, do not delay.

(Ps 40:17)

We wait in faith.

"Tarrying with the negative"

The great philosopher Hegel said:

> "Death ... is of all things the most dreadful, and to hold fast to what is dead requires the greatest strength. Lacking strength, Beauty hates the Understanding for asking of her what it cannot do. But the life of Spirit is not the life that shrinks from death and keeps itself untouched by devastation, but rather the life that endures it and maintains itself in it. It wins its truth only when, in utter dismemberment, it finds itself. It is this power, not as something positive, which closes its eyes to the negative, as when we say of something that it is nothing or is false, and then, having done with it, turn away and pass on to something else; on the contrary, Spirit is this power only by

looking the negative in the face, and tarrying with it. This tarrying with the negative is the magical power that converts it into being."[2]

We grow in the Spirit not by turning our eyes from the negative in our world and ourselves. Many of our problems come from trying to run away from these. Hegel tells us to "tarry" with the negativeness. We grow by facing the real not by denial. Qoheleth found the world to be different from what he once believed. He put down in writing his feelings about this. In doing this he helps us express our negativity. He gives voice to it. When we "tarry" with him we begin to grow beyond the negative. We grow in the Spirit by accepting the negative and allowing the light in.

Qoheleth speaks of the futility of our striving. In a haunting and melancholy poem (1:3-11) he poses a famous question: "What do we get from all our toil?" The answer is "nothing". In nature's wordless reward there is nothing but futility.

"What do people gain from all the toil
at which they toil under the sun?
    A generation goes, and a generation comes,
but the earth remains forever.
    The sun rises and the sun goes down,
and hurries to the place where it rises.
    The wind blows to the south,
and goes around to the north;
round and round goes the wind,
and on its circuits the wind returns.
    All streams run to the sea,
but the sea is not full;
to the place where the streams flow,
there they continue to flow.
    All things are wearisome;
more than one can express;

[2] G. W. F. Hegel, Phenomenology of Spirit, translated by A.V. Miller (Oxford: 1977), p. 19 (§32).

the eye is not satisfied with seeing,
or the ear filled with hearing.
    What has been is what will be,
and what has been done is what will be done;
there is nothing new under the sun.
    Is there a thing of which it is said,
"See, this is new"?
It has already been,
in the ages before us.
    The people of long ago are not remembered,
nor will there be any remembrance
of people yet to come
by those who come after them.

                                (Ecclesiastes 1:3-11)

He speaks of *'amal'*, toil, of a humble righteous person would be rewarded somehow. All this work is done under the sun. The Teacher draws on four elements of ancient cosmology – earth (v.4), the fire of the sun (v.5), wind (v.6) and water (v.7) – to describe cycles of inevitability that touch upon nature. The sun rises eastwards and sets again only to begin all over again. Streams rush to the sea and the sea is never full. All is predictable. There is "nothing new under the sun" (v.9). Some claim that they have something new only to find it has always been around. We become exhausted with the monotonous futility of it all. The passage concludes with the devastating assertion that the memory of people past, present and future will fail as well (v.11). His view of the world is bleak and lacks vitality. It is a state we reach when we face disappointment and fall out of love. The world is bleak and we see the negative. "All is vanity and chasing of the wind" (1:14). He says:

"I saw all the deeds that are done under the sun;
and see, all is vanity and a chasing after wind.
    What is crooked cannot be made straight,
and what is lacking cannot be counted."

                                  (1:14-15)

The word for wind is the same as the word for spirit. The chasing of the wind conveys the idea of searching and hoping, but all the time he feels everything is futile. This is an experience of negativity that Qoheleth puts words on. It helps us to see how things work. In staying with the feeling ("tarrying" in Hegel's words) we come to an acceptance of the way we feel and at the same time we hope that one day the Holy Spirit will lead us to a better day. It is in these negative situations that we meet God. Qoheleth's idea of nothing new under the sun should prod us to think. We see now that things do change. The world of climate change shows us that nature does change. We however can make a difference in this. We can take responsibility.

When things seem futile we place before ourselves the cross. St. Paul tells us: "For the message of the cross is foolishness to those that are perishing, but to us who are being saved it is the power of God" (1 Cor 1:18) and later he says "…we proclaim Christ crucified, a stumbling block to Jews and foolishness to Gentiles" (1 Cor 1:23) but "God's foolishness is wiser then human wisdom" (1 Cor 1:24). To the world the death of Jesus seemed an absolute catastrophe, a complete and utter failure. It seemed utterly futile. But God caused Jesus to rise from the dead and conquer death. Through him God poured out the Holy Spirit. The Holy Spirit dwells in us. We are his temples (1 Cor 6:19). "Whoever is united with the Lord is one with him in Spirit" (1 Cor 6:17). We realise that Jesus is alive in God and we are called to be one with him. He gives meaning to our suffering and in his unique way he uses our suffering to heal the broken world and those who are broken in it. In human reckoning our efforts are futile and "chasing of the wind". Qoheleth tells us this. However, when we turn to God in Jesus and focus on him, he comes to us and dwells in us. In silence we can wait and hope. God will reveal himself in us in a moment of silence and we feel renewed. Qoheleth's words show us our fear. In turning to Jesus we learn that God's ways are infinitely different from our ordinary, worldly thinking.

Hemingway, a modern Qoheleth

Ernest Hemingway (+1961) was an American novelist, short-story writer and journalist. He wrote in an economical and understated style. He called this the iceberg theory. There was a lot going on beneath the surface. He was born in Oak Park, Illinois. He became a reporter for 'The Kansas City Star'. He left for the Italian front in World War I, to work as an ambulance driver. In 1918 he was seriously wounded and this experience formed the basis for his novel 'A Farewell to Arms'. He was an explorer and adventurer. He almost died in 1954 after two plane crashes on successive days. He suffered severe injuries and ill health for the rest of his life. In 1959 he bought a house in Ketchum, Idaho. Here he took his life in 1961. His father Clarence had taken his life in 1928 and this event haunted Hemingway for the rest of his life. He was prone to the same depressive illness as his father. In happier times as a young man Hemingway had enjoyed fishing, hunting and camping with his father and this gave him a love for the outdoors and adventure.

'A Clean, Well-Lighted Place' was a short story written by Hemingway and published in Scribner's Magazine in 1933. It shows a deaf old man who is the sole patron of a cafe. Nearby two waiters, one young, one old, talk about him. The waiters speculate about the old man's recent suicide attempt. The old man orders another brandy but the young waiter tells him no, the place is closed. He wants to rush home. The older waiter is more thoughtful. He muses on youth and observes he is one "of those who like to stay late in the cafe," likening himself to the old man. He thinks of the importance for some people of having "a clean, well-lighted place" in which they can spend time. After the young waiter leaves, the older man reflects on the emptiness of his own life and returns to his home and his insomnia. Hemingway was quoted as saying this might be his favourite story.[3]

When the owner finds himself alone he finds he is fearful – but of what?

> What did he fear? It was not fear or dread. it was a nothing
> that he knew too well. It was all a nothing and a man was
> nothing too. It was only that and light was all it needed and
> a certain cleanness and order.[4]

[3] A. E. Hotchner, Papa Hemingway (London: 1966), p. 141. James Joyce said it was one of the best short stories ever written [lost generation website].
[4] E. Hemingway, A Clean, Well-Lighted Place in Complete Short Stories of Ernest Hemingway (London: 1987), p. 291.

This feeling of 'nothingness' echoes Qoheleth. He used the word *'hebel'* which we translated as 'vanity' and can also mean 'emptiness' or 'nothingness'. The owner feels a deep emptiness as if he were nothing. He is supremely lonely. That is what he is afraid of. When the place he worked is clean, well-lighted and there are people about, he can keep this feeling at bay, but now he can't. He finds life empty – nothing and again nothing, *'nada y pues nada y nada y pues nada'*. *'Nada'* means 'nothing'. It is Qoheleth's *'hebel'* He expresses a prayer of emptiness...

"Our nada who art in nada"
(A Clean, Well-Lighted Place, p. 292)

He is one of the many lonely people who live in our world who feel they are worthless. They are like 'Daisy' who we met in Chapter One. The word he uses for nothing is 'nada'. This is the word used by John of the Cross. He refers to the 'Dark Night of the Soul'. The 'nothing' we feel is the night when God works. God is at work in the night of loneliness. We are not alone. Simone Weil tells us that in this dark night of loneliness we should accept the emptiness and loneliness because from the emptiness comes new life and healing.

In his novel 'A Farewell to Arms' Hemingway uses the word 'nada' as well. This novel was published in 1929. It tells the story of an American, Frederic Henry, who served as a lieutenant (Italian: tenente) in the ambulance corps of the Italian Army. It describes the love affair between Henry and an English nurse, Catherine Barkley. Frederic Henry narrates the story. The inspiration was based on Agnes von Kurowsky, a nurse who cared for Hemingway in a hospital in Milan after he had been wounded. However the love affair did not work out. The unnamed priest was based on Don Giuseppe Bianchi, the priest Hemingway met on the front and he was impressed by him. When he was wounded Don Giuseppe ministered to him and the other wounded. Hemingway spoke of being anointed by Don Giuseppe. This was before he formally became a Catholic. Hemingway said:

"If I am anything I am a Catholic. Had extreme unction administered to me as such in July 1918 and recovered...

It is most certainly the most comfortable religion for anyone soldiering. Am not what is called a "good" Catholic... But cannot imagine taking any other religion seriously."

[included in Michael Reynolds, Hemingway:
The Paris Years (New York: 1999)]

In one scene Catherine gives Frederic a little picture of Saint Anthony to keep him safe. He asks her if she is a Catholic. She tells him she isn't but she felt protected with her little Saint Anthony and now she was giving this to Frederic before he returned to the front. He put the chain with the little picture of Saint Anthony around his neck. It was a token of love. In little scenes like this we see Hemingway's Iceberg Theory. There is what we see on the surface but there is a lot more beneath the surface. Catherine is not a Catholic but she is sympathetic and a searcher. She shares what is precious to her to protect Frederic.[5]

In Book 5 of 'A Farewell to Arms' Catherine and Frederic have escaped the war and now live in a wooden house on a mountain outside the village of Montreux. Catherine is pregnant and they agree to move to Lausanne to be closer to a hospital. Catherine goes into labour and is taken to hospital where she undergoes a Caesarean operation. Catherine starts haemorrhaging and she dies in Frederic's arms. Hemingway communicates Frederic's sadness in the following words using his Iceberg Theory:

"It was the only thing to do," he said. "The operation proved—"
"I do not want to talk about it," I said.
"I would like to take you to your hotel."
"No, thank you."
He went down the hall. I went to the door of the room.
"You can't come in now," one of the nurses said.
"Yes I can," I said.
"You can't come in yet."

[5] Ernest Hemingway, A Farewell to Arms (New York: 1929).

"You get out," I said. "The other one too."
But after I had got them out and shut the door and turned off the light it wasn't any good. it was like saying goodbye to a statue. After a while I went out and left the hospital and walked back to the hotel in the rain.

The short conversation with the surgeon, the brief account of walking home in the rain are used to tell us that deep down there are feelings of grief and loss. There is a profound loneliness. Beneath the iceberg there is a lot going on. This is Hemingway's way of writing. We can feel the rain and the loneliness of the scene.

Earlier in the book Frederic had thought of the loneliness of the world and how the good suffer. He said:

> "If people bring so much courage to this world the world has to kill them to break them, so of course it kills them. The world breaks every one and afterward many are strong at the broken places. But those that will not break it kills. It kills the very good and the very gentle and the very brave impartially. If you are none of these you can be sure it will kill you too but there will be no special hurry."

He has a sad view of the way things are especially after his experience. He has a sense of loneliness and loss. This helps us understand Qoheleth. His view of life is negative because of his experience. They put words on how it feels to be helpless and alone. They put words on what it feels like to see the good suffer and those who do evil prosper. These are experiences many go through. In reading Qoheleth and Hemingway we can name the feelings we go through. Life can be very cruel. In reading these writers we can come to understand and accept this.

'The Old Man and the Sea' is a novella written by Hemingway in 1951 in Cayo Blanco (Cuba) and published in 1952. It tells the story of an aging Cuban fisherman who struggles with a giant marlin far out in the Gulf Stream off the coast of Cuba. The fisherman's name is Santiago.

He is now seen as "salado" – the worst form of unlucky. Manolin, a young man that Santiago trained, has been told by his parents to go to a different boat because they are lucky. Manolin visits his friend by night and they talk about baseball and Santiago's favourite player, Joe DiMaggio.

Santiago heads out again. He sees a giant marlin. The story centres with Santiago catching the giant fish far away from the shore. The trail of blood attracts sharks and Santiago fights them off as best he could, but in the end they win. They eat the marlin.

When Santiago returns to the village he sleeps. But the other fishermen who had mocked Santiago now look in awe at what Santiago had done. When Santiago awakes he donates the head to Pedrico, a fellow fisherman, who had been kind to Santiago. Santiago sleeps but now in peace. He had come to a new peace with himself.

Life, the possibility of renewal, follow on the heels of death in the novella. The book's crucifixion imagery emphasises the cyclical connection between life and death, as does Santiago's battle with the marlin. His bringing home of the marlin earns the respect of the fishermen who had mocked him and restores the companionship of Manolin who is now with him again. He has achieved an inner peace. On the face of it Santiago failed but he had come to a new peace. Santiago said "But man is not made to endure defeat... A man can be destroyed, but not defeated."[6]

It was in writing that Hemingway moved forward with life. In writing he worked through with his characters their fears and disappointments. He admitted he was a "peculiar Catholic".[7] He always explained the seriousness of true prayers. In a letter to Bernard Berenson he explains how the prayers of sinners are powerful (4 May 1953). We can recall here Charles Péguy's famous statement – used as the epigraph in Graham Greene's novel 'The Heart of the Matter':

[6] Ernest Hemingway, The Old Man and the Sea (Delhi, India: 2022 ed.), p. 61.
[7] Michael Reynolds, Hemingway: The Final Years (New York: 1999), p. 238.

"The sinner lies at the very heart of Christianity…. Again, no one is more competent than a sinner in matters of Christianity. No one, unless it be a saint"

(Charles Péguy; Basic Verities)

Chapter 3

Can You Hear Me?

For Qoheleth God is absent on a personal level. He has a picture of god far away and a babbling, small man far away from God. We read:

> Guard your steps when you go to the house of God. Go near
> to listen rather than to offer the sacrifice of fools, who do
> not know that they do wrong.
> Do not be quick with your mouth,
>   do not be hasty in your heart
>   to utter anything before God.
> God is in heaven
>   and you are on earth,
>   so let your words be few.
>
> (Ecc 5:1-2)

Qoheleth begins with a theme that was common to the prophets. In the Book of Samuel we read: "Does the Lord take pleasure in burnt offerings and sacrifices as much as in obeying the Lord? To obey is better than sacrifice, to pay attention is better than the fat of rams" (1 Sam 15:22). To enter the temple demands that the one entering live a proper life. We find this in Amos (5:21-25), Hosea (6:6), Isaiah (ch. 1), Micah (6:6-8) and Jeremiah (ch. 7). We find this theme in the Wisdom literature (Psalm 50; Sirach 34:18-35:10). Otherwise the insincere sacrifice will become a source of judgement on the insincere one. We should be careful of the words we use. We should use a few and mean what we say.

Qoheleth's view of God is fearful and negative. We are poor and God lives far away from us. We read in the psalms "The heaven, even the heavens are the Lord's: but the earth he has given to the children of men" (Ps 115:16). So Qoheleth advises us to use few words. He tells us: "Man is a poor vain creature, all he is and has is vanity…" (Ecc 6:11) and later he says: "The words of a wise man are gracious; but the lips of a fool will swallow up himself" (Ecc 10:12). Because there is distance between ourselves and God we should respect this according to Qoheleth. The answer to Qoheleth lies in Jesus. He is God among us – the "emmanuel" (Matthew 1:23). Jesus tells us of the care of the Father for us. He tells us: "And when you pray do not keep babbling like the pagans, for they think they will be heard because of many words. Do not be like them, for your father knows what you need before you ask him" (Matthew 6:7-8) and he tells us "Come to me all you who labour and are overburdened and I will give you rest" (Matthew 11:28).

Lord can you hear me?

Damien Rice is an Irish singer-songwriter. He began his career with a band called "Juniper". He left the band in 1998 and worked as a farmer in Tuscany and busked throughout Europe before returning to Ireland in 2001 when he began a solo career. 'O' was his debut album. It was dedicated to Rice's friend Mic Christopher who died of a head injury in 2001. Music speaks to the heart in ways we don't understand. Rice's words and music speak to us and contain our struggles.

One of the songs on the album is called 'Cold Water' in which he dueled with Lisa Hannigan. He says:

> "Cold, cold water surrounds me now
> And all I've got is your hand
> Lord, can you hear me now?
> Lord, can you hear me now?
> Lord, can you hear me now?
> Or am I lost?

He captures the fear many feel. We worry we do not matter. The fear of being lost can overcome us. We often don't believe in ourselves or our value. This is the reason we don't believe in God – we feel we are not loved or lovable. We feel like Daisy. We feel invisible and of no account. Music can express our fears.

The singer cries out:

> "Oh, I love you
> Don't you know I love you and I always have?
> Hallelujah
> Will you come with me?

We long for God's love but we feel fear. "Lord (can you hear me now?)".

Another band who expresses in music our feelings is 'Coldplay'. They were formed in London in 1997. 'Fix You' is a song written by Chris Martin of 'Coldplay'. He wrote the song to comfort his then wife Gwyneth Paltrow after her father died. The songs contains an organ accompaniment. The words are:

> "When you try your best, but you don't succeed
> When you get what you want, but not what you need
> When you feel so tired, but you can't sleep
> Stuck in reverse
> And the tears come streaming down your face
> When you lose something you can't replace
> When you love someone, but it goes to waste
> Could it be worse?
>
> Lights will guide you home
> And ignite your bones
> And I will try to fix you"

Through the song and its words he shares in the pain of Gwyneth Paltrow. One time some young friends of Beethoven lost their child. Beethoven visited the couple. He said nothing but played a beautiful and sad piece of music. That was his way of sharing their pain. Similarly with Chris Martin and 'Coldplay':

> "Tears stream down your face
> When you lose something you cannot replace
> Tears stream down your face and I"

38

Nick Cave is an Australian singer. He has been called a "Goth God". In his music he wrestles with faith, doubt, loneliness, grief and loss. In his song 'Into My Arms' he says:

> "I don't believe in an interventionist God
> But I know, darling, that you do
> But if I did I would kneel down and ask Him
> Not to intervene when it came to you
> Not to touch a hair on your head
> To leave you as you are
> And if He felt He had to direct you
> Then direct you into my arms
>
> Into my arms, O Lord
> Into my arms, O Lord
> Into my arms, O Lord
> Into my arms"

God seems far away as in Qoheleth. But he wrestles with this God. Later on in the song he says:

> "But I believe in love
> And I know that you do too
> And I believe in some kind of path
> That we can walk down, me and you
> So keep your candles burning
> And make her journey bright and pure
> That she will keep returning
> Always and evermore"

Cave said he wrote the song in Rehab,

> "I was actually walking back from church through the fields, and the tune came into my head, and when I got back to the facility I sat down at the cranky old piano and wrote the melody and chords, then went up to the dormitory, sat on my bed and wrote these lyrics."[1]

---

[1] Nick Cave and Sean O'Hagan, Faith, Hope and Carnage (New York: 2022), p. 51.

He performed this song at the funeral of INXS singer, Michael Hutchence. The melancholic lyrics of 'Into My Arms' Cave attributed to the breakup of his longterm relationship with Vivienne Carneiro.

In 2015 Cave's son Arthur experimented with LSD and fell from a cliff at Ovingdean, near Brighton. Cave explored the effect of Arthur's death on his family in the 2016 documentary film 'One More Time With Feeling', the 2016 album 'Skeleton Time' and the 2019 album 'Ghosteen'. Cave is a man who prays, goes to Mass and reads his Bible. He does not present us with a theology but a man who sincerely seeks God in the face of loss, loneliness and grief. In 2022 he issued a book called 'Faith, Hope and Carnage' – a set of interviews with Sean O'Hagan.

'Stranger Then Kindness' is a book Nick Cave issued in 2020.[2] It is a journey in images and words of the creative work of Nick Cave. It is accompanied by commentary and meditations from Cave himself, Janine Barrand and Darcey Steinke.

'God is in the House' is a song by Nick Cave. It has hope that God is here even in the confusion.

> "Well-meaning little therapists
> Goose-stepping twelve-stepping Tetotalitarianists
> The tipsy, the reeling and the drop down pissed
> We got no time for that stuff here
> Zero crime and no fear
> We've bred all our kittens white
> So you can see them in the night
> And at night we're on our knees
> As quiet as a mouse
> Since the word got out
> From the North down to the South
> For no-one's left in doubt

---

[2] Nick Cave, Stranger Than Kindness (Edinburgh: 2020).

There's no fear about
If we all hold hands and very quietly shout
Hallelujah
God is in the house
God is in the house
Oh I wish He would come out
God is in the house"

He wishes to see the God we worship and his love come to bear in the confusion and brokenness of reality. Darcey Steinke in 'Stranger Than Kindness' describes how she lived in a house near William Faulkner's home in Oxford, Mississippi. She called the meditation 'God is in the House'. She spoke of the tourists who came to Faulkner's house. They could see a manuscript copy of 'A Fable'. One tourist who stuck in her mind was a young Japanese boy who wore a Nick Cave and The Bad Seeds t-shirt. She thought of why people like him were drawn to Faulkner's house. She thought of Cave's questions. She quotes him:

> 'What goes on up there,' Cave writes in And the Ass Saw
> the Angel, 'what measure the affliction? What weight the
> iron? Is it a chance system? ... or – anti-creation, something
> seasonal, something astrological?'
>
> (Stranger Than Kindness, p. 44)

Both Faulkner's and Cave's characters reside in paradox, filled with doubt, longing, questions and frustration. "All the best people ... are dinged up a little" (Stranger Than Kindness, p. 46). Our flaws and scars go to make us up. It is in the darkness that we meet God. We seek God and his healing. Faulkner and Cave show us our brokenness but this is part of us and here we find our need for love. The songs and words can express our brokenness and they cry out to God for healing. When we are overcome with the feeling of shame and guilt we think we are far from God, but the truth is God is even closer to us than we are to ourselves and this includes the times of our guilt and shame. Jesus says: "It is not the healthy who need a doctor, but the sick. I have not come to call the righteous, but sinners" (Mark 2:17).

These songs call to mind the psalms of lament. Dermot Cox said the words of these psalms form a kind of sacrament.[3] We meet God in the words even though the words seem to say we are far away. One such psalm is Psalm 6. We read...

> LORD, do not rebuke me in your anger or discipline me in your wrath.
> Have mercy on me, LORD, for I am faint; heal me, LORD, for my bones are in agony.
> My soul is in deep anguish. How long, LORD, how long?
> Turn, LORD, and deliver me; save me because of your unfailing love.
> Among the dead no one proclaims your name. Who praises you from the grave?
> I am worn out from my groaning. All night long I flood my bed with weeping and drench my couch with tears.
> My eyes grow weak with sorrow; they fail because of all my foes.

The soul is in agony, like the agony expressed in our brief look at the modern songs. He is worn out with sadness. His soul is in deep anguish. He cries out "How long, Lord, how long". These psalms influenced Bono of U2.

The words are where we meet God. We trust him with our loneliness, fear and doubt. This explains the change in the psalm...

> Away from me, all you who do evil,
>   for the LORD has heard my weeping.
> The LORD has heard my cry for mercy;
>   the LORD accepts my prayer.
> All my enemies will be overwhelmed with shame and anguish;
>   they will turn back and suddenly be put to shame.

---

[3] Dermot Cox, The Psalms in the Life of God's People (Slough: 1984).

Through the words of the psalm, which is a prayer, he finds peace. This is because he knows after meeting God he is not alone. His tears are not lost. He has become himself again. When we embark on this journey we hope to find this peace. Our modern songwriters continue the tradition of lament we find in the Psalms of Lament.

In the meantime we need to wait patiently as Ps 27 tells us:

> "Wait for the Lord.
> Be strong and don't lose hope.
> Wait for the Lord."

(Psalm 27:14)

Chapter 4

Little Happiness

"The best people possess a feeling for beauty, the courage to take risks, the discipline to tell the truth, the capacity for sacrifice. Ironically, their virtues make them vulnerable; they are often wounded, sometimes destroyed."

            – Ernest Hemingway

Qoheleth finds little happiness but no joy. He seems to arrive at a sombre happiness. In chapter 2 he says:

> I said to myself, "Come now, I will test you with pleasure to find out what is good." But that also proved to be meaningless. "Laughter," I said, "is madness. And what does pleasure accomplish?" I tried cheering myself with wine, and embracing folly—my mind still guiding me with wisdom. I wanted to see what was good for people to do under the heavens during the few days of their lives.
>
>   (Ecc 2:1-3)

Before this he has reasoned that wisdom is an absurdity, 'vanity'. He finds pleasure an absurdity as well. He goes on to try and find fulfillment in property, produce, wealth and sex. He finds all empty and useless.

> I denied myself nothing my eyes desired;
>   I refused my heart no pleasure.
> My heart took delight in all my labor,
>   and this was the reward for all my toil.
>   Yet when I surveyed all that my hands had done
>   and what I had toiled to achieve,
> everything was meaningless, a chasing after the wind;
>   nothing was gained under the sun.
>
>   (Ecc 2:10f)

He looked on the work he had done. This too was vanity and chasing of the wind. There was no enduring sense of meaning to his life for all the earthly achievements and accomplishments.

Qoheleth later has good things about 'simhah' (happiness) and seeing good. He says pleasure is "good" (3:12; 2; 5:17; 8:15). It is man's "portion" (2:10; 3:22; 5:17; 9:9) allocated and approved by God (2:24,26; 3:13; 5:18; 9:7). He says pleasure is the best thing in life (3:22). He goes on to say it is the only good thing.

In chapter 9 he says:

> So I reflected on all this and concluded that the righteous and the wise and what they do are in God's hands, but no one knows whether love or hate awaits them. All share a common destiny—the righteous and the wicked, the good and the bad, the clean and the unclean, those who offer sacrifices and those who do not.
>
> As it is with the good,
>   so with the sinful;
> as it is with those who take oaths,
>   so with those who are afraid to take them.
> This is the evil in everything that happens under the sun: The same destiny overtakes all. The hearts of people, moreover, are full of evil and there is madness in their hearts while they live, and afterward they join the dead. Anyone who is among the living has hope—even a live dog is better off than a dead lion!
>
> For the living know that they will die,
>   but the dead know nothing;
> they have no further reward,
>   and even their name is forgotten.
> Their love, their hate
>   and their jealousy have long since vanished;
> never again will they have a part
>   in anything that happens under the sun.

Go, eat your food with gladness, and drink your wine with
a joyful heart, for God has already approved what you do.
Always be clothed in white, and always anoint your head
with oil. Enjoy life with your wife, whom you love, all the
days of this meaningless life that God has given you under
the sun—all your meaningless days. For this is your lot in
life and in your toilsome labor under the sun. Whatever
your hand finds to do, do it with all your might, for in the
realm of the dead, where you are going, there is neither
working nor planning nor knowledge nor wisdom.

(9:1-10)

The love and hate that await us see the attitude of God though we cannot
know the divine verdict in advance. The same fate of death awaits
everyone – the good and bad. In the time of Qoheleth there wasn't a
belief in the afterlife. The advantage of the living human being
deteriorates into the pain of knowing what lies ahead. In the Wisdom of
Solomon we read:

Our name will be forgotten in time,
and no one will remember our works;
our life will pass away like the traces of a cloud
and be scattered like mist
that is chased by the rays of the sun
and overcome by its heat.
For our allotted time is the passing of a shadow,
and there is no return from our death,
because it is sealed up and no one turns back.

(Wisdom 2:4-5)

He does tell us to find joy in all our endeavors while we can. He tells us
it is morally good to enjoy bread, wine and life itself. In the face of this
we still have to face death. We are to be consigned to Sheol – this is a
place of darkness where the dead go. This was a form of subterranean
underworld where the dead went. Even in his praise of happiness there
is the shadow of gloom. Yet in the face of absurdity ("vanity") we can

46

still enjoy whatever moments of joy we can. The Book of Proverbs puts it well:

> "Even in merriment the heart may ache…"
>
> (Prov 14:13)

'Secular Parables'

Jesus' resurrection is the answer to Qoheleth. In the Song of Songs we read: "Love is as strong as death" (Song 8:6). In the resurrection we see love is stronger than death. he has conquered death and will not die. He has poured out his Holy Spirit as well. When we live "in Christ" all of our lives have value. It also enables us to see all as gift.

Karl Barth takes seriously the claim that "Jesus is the Light of Life." He says:

> "If with the prophets and apostles we have our starting-point at His resurrection and therefore at His revelation as the One who was and is and will be; if we recognise and confess Him as the One who was and is and will be, then we recognise and confess that not we alone, nor the community which, following the prophets and apostles, believes in Him and loves Him and hopes in Him, but de jure all men and all creation derive from His cross, from the reconciliation accomplished in Him, and are ordained to be the theatre of His glory and therefore the recipients and bearers of His Word. In the very light of this narrower sphere of the Bible and the Church, we cannot possibly think that He cannot speak, and His speech cannot be attested, outside this sphere. (p. 117)[1]

He goes on to suggest that the Spirit of God is the source of all truth and he even says that occurrences in our world can be a source of revelation.

[1] Karl Barth, Church Dogmatics: The Doctrine of Reconciliation IV.3.1 (Edinburgh: 1961), p. 117.

God shows forth himself in events in our world. He describes how the goodness of creation can point us to the creator:

> ...does this authentically if and as and to the extent that what it says individually and specifically is only apparently and at a first hearing an abstraction, but really declares the goodness, peril, triumph and future glory of the divine work of creation which is enclosed in Jesus Christ...so that...it really declares the totality of this work....
>
> (Church Dogmatics, p. 123)

Events in our world can lead us to praise God. One of the ways Barth was inspired to praise God was the music of Mozart. He allowed human beings to pay attention to God's glory. An appreciation for the beauty and richness of Mozart's music developed over time. It coincided with Barth's appreciation of the incarnation. Mozart's music for him was a liberating experience. It showed him God's promise to preserve creation and his praise of a transformation of all creation. In the face of the world's 'no', there is always the divine 'yes'. Mozart intended this to be the divine 'yes' according to Barth. Only God can bear the thought of nothingness and deliver on the promise to make humanity free. Mozart affirmed Barth's belief in God's final victory. He sees Mozart's music as a celebration of creation and of eschatological hope. Eschatology refers to our hope for a new creation where all tears will be wiped away (Rev 21:4).

Amadeus

Wolfgang Amadeus Mozart (+1791) was a prolific and influential composer of the classical period. he was born in Salzburg, then in the Roman Empire. He showed prodigious ability from his earliest childhood. He began composing from the age of three and he performed before European royalty. Once, as a child in court at Vienna, he slipped on the floor and a young Marie-Antoinette picked him up. The very young Mozart proposed to her on the spot. His father brought him on three trips to Italy. At 17 he was a musician in the Salzburg court but he grew restless and travelled in search of a better position.

While visiting Vienna in 1781, Mozart was dismissed from his Salzburg position. He stayed in Vienna, where he achieved fame but little financial security. During his years there, he composed many of his best know symphonies, concertos and operas. His Requiem was largely unfinished by the time of his death at the age of 35. The exact circumstances of his death are unknown and has become the source of much mythology. He has, according to Barth, an intuitive childlike awareness of the presence of God in all creation. He says:

> "Beautiful playing presupposes an intuitive, childlike awareness of the essence or center–as also the beginnings and the end–of all things. It is from this center, from this beginning and end, that I hear Mozart created his music. I can hear those boundaries which he imposed upon himself because it was precisely this discipline that gave him joy. And when I hear him, it gladdens, encourages, and comforts me as well."[2]

Barth's appreciation of the beauty of Mozart's music led him to appreciate God's beauty. In this way Mozart's music was a form of "secular parable". Sometimes Mozart's music gives us sheer delight. In other portions like the death music at the end of Don Giovanni we are moved by the tragedy that is set before us. Mozart can write on all these dimensions. In his 'Marriage of Figaro' he shows the plight of ordinary people unlike operas which up to this had been written about the rich and powerful. In doing this he found himself opposed to Salieri. This rivalry was dramatized in the film 'Amadeus' (1984) directed by Milos Forman. It is a fictionalised story of Mozart and Salieri. Mozart's music forms the backdrop to the film.

Hans Kung was influenced by Barth and his work on Mozart. He pointed out cheekily that Barth seemed almost apologetic about Mozart's Catholicism. Mozart's writings are full of references to God the Creator, his confidence in Christ's promises and his attachment to the "mystical sanctuary of our religion" – the Eucharist. Much of his faith came from his father, Leopold Mozart, who received twelve years of education by

---

[2] Karl Barth, Wolfang Amadeus Mozart (Eugene, Oregon: 1986), p. 150.

the Jesuits, studied theology and philosophy and he paid attention to Mozart's religious formation. When his father was dying Wolfgang told him: "I thank God for graciously granting me the opportunity ... of learning that death is the key that unlocks the door to our true happiness."

In the second half of Kung's book on Mozart Kung goes on to say that Mozart's music for religious settings was "not just music at worship but music of worship, an exegesis of liturgy."[3] The vehicle through which Kung makes his case is Mozart's Coronation Mass, most likely performed on Easter Sunday, 1779. Kung says:

> "No, this music is the liturgy itself, ringing out in festal sound, and it gives musical expression to the subject matter, the liturgical text itself. So all in all this is liturgical music which expounds the text, and in its beauty, purity and perfection it already gives us a glimpse of the eternal, joyful sound of the spheres with their eternal Glorias: the *vita venturi saeculi*, the "life of the world to come," which is confessed at the end of the *Credo*."

The sense of wonder conveyed by Mozart's music and his liturgical music is influenced by Mozart's awareness of the divine, the transcendent. His music of the Coronation was an affair of the heart and was an expression of his deep love for God.

Hans Urs Von Balthasar (+1988) was a close friend of Barth. He and Barth were at the University of Basel. Barth was a professor there and Von Balthasar the chaplain. Von Balthasar found himself at an impasse in his theological thought. He brought his problems to Barth who guided him through his problems. This was a great release for Von Balthasar.[4]

Von Balthasar was a Swiss theologian and one who is considered as one of the most important of the 20th century. He shared with Barth a love of the music of Mozart. He said music represents: "...the dynamism of

---

[3] Hans Kung, Mozart: Traces of Transcendence (London: 1992).

[4] see Podcast by D. Stephen Long; also his book, Saving Karl Barth: Vol Balthasar's Preoccupation (Minneapolis: 2014).

God, precisely beyond the intellectual visible, verbal dimension, an immediate pure form of truth."[5] Von Balthasar says that all "art tends to the perfect experience or realisation of a spiritual idea" (lo Sviluppo, 13-15). Music approximates to the truth and beauty of God.

> "The truth, which is thought, becomes, in its material dimension, beauty. This latter aspect is therefore only an analogical expression of the truth, and both are identical, inasmuch as they designate the divine."
>
> (lo Sviluppo, p. 37)

He goes on to speak of how music moves us even in ways we do not fully understand...

> "Music is the most incomprehensible art because it is the most immediate one. It questions us more directly, penetrating deeper in us than the others. But is it not perhaps this closeness that makes it an eternal enigma, which has always moved us to fix its limits, to regulate it, to force it into numbers and express it endlessly in laws?"
>
> (lo Sviluppo, p. 13)

He speaks of Mozart whom he loved, like his friend Barth. He said we could hear the echo of creation transfigured and redeemed:

> "Mozart serves by making audible the triumphal hymn of a prelapsarian and resurrected creation, in which suffering and guilt are not presented as faint memory, as past, but as conquered, absolved, transfigured present."

Von Balthasar looks at inspiration to help us understand the Holy Spirit: "The artist is never more free than when he feels inspired to work. Mozart's 'Magic Flute' is an inspired work of this kind."

In Jesus we are accepted, loved, healed and forgiven. His resurrection is the beginning of God's final victory over all the brokenness and evil of

---

[5] Hans Urs Von Balthasar, Pierangelo Sequeri (trans.), Lo Sviluppo dell'idea musicale (Milan: 1995), p. 13-15.

the world. From the luminosity and brilliance of the work of Mozart, Von Balthasar sees the music of Mozart as a celebration of creation and future hope. This does not mean that Mozart rationally came to do this. It came naturally from his creative genius. Barth gave the name 'secular parable' to this event.

Praise of all creation:

C. S. Lewis thought Psalm 19 was one of the greatest poems in the Psalter. He sees the beauty and splendour of the Hebrew poetry found in the Psalter. The psalm begins:

> The heavens declare the glory of God;
>> the skies proclaim the work of his hands.
> Day after day they pour forth speech;
>> night after night they reveal knowledge.
> They have no speech, they use no words;
>> no sound is heard from them.
> Yet their voice goes out into all the earth,
>> their words to the ends of the world.
> In the heavens God has pitched a tent for the sun.
> It is like a bridegroom coming out of his chamber,
>> like a champion rejoicing to run his course.
> It rises at one end of the heavens
>> and makes its circuit to the other;
>> nothing is deprived of its warmth.
>
> (Ps 19:1-6)

The psalmist saw the glory of God reflected in the Heavens. He sees the beauty of God in all things. "The firmament" shows God's handiwork. The day sky and the night sky reveal for us the glory, wisdom, beauty and creative greatness of God. "There is no speech nor language" yet their voice is heard. The beginning of Ps 19 calls us to praise God in all things. All speak of his glory if we have eyes to see. This is the same experience Von Balthasar and Barth had before Mozart's music. Qoheleth saw all good things coming to an end but now in the light of the Resurrection and the Holy Spirit all beauty speaks of God and our continued life in him.

The 'Canticle of the Sun' is a song written by Saint Francis of Assisi (+1226). The 'Canticle of the Sun' thanks God for his creation and thanks him for such creations of "brother sun" and "sister water". He is said to have composed most of the canticle in late 1224 while he was ill at San Damiano. He could no longer see the things he praised because he was now blind. Pope Francis called his encyclical 'Laudato Si' after the Canticle. The Canticle begins as follows

> Most High, all-powerful, good Lord,
> Yours are the praises, the glory, the honor, and all blessings.
> To You alone, Most High, do they belong,
> and no man is worthy to mention Your name.
> Praised be You, my Lord, with all your creatures;
> especially Brother Sun, who is the day, and through whom
>   You give us light.
> And he is beautiful and radiant with great splendor,
> and bears a likeness to You, Most High One.
> Praised be You, my Lord, through Sister Moon and the
>   stars;
> in heaven You formed them clear and precious and
>   beautiful.

All joy comes from God and leads us back to him. It calls us to him and in him is eternal life.

Chapter 5

Time

T. S. Eliot said

> "Time for you and time for me
> And time yet for a hundred indecisions
> And for a hundred visions and revisions
> Before the taking of tea and toast."

This comes from T. S. Eliot's poem "The Love Song of J. Alfred Prufrock". Prufrock laments his physical and intellectual inertia, the lost opportunities of his life and lack of spiritual progress and is haunted by reminders of unattained love. With visceral feelings of weariness, regret, embarrassment, longing, frustration, a sense of decay, Prufrock has become one of the most recognised voices in literature. He says:

> "I grow old... I grow old
> I shall wear the bottoms of my trousers rolled"

The emptiness of life is typified by the "women who come and go / Talking of Michelangelo." He expresses the same world-weariness as Qoheleth.

In one of the most quoted passages from Qoheleth we read:

> There is a time for everything,
>   and a season for every activity under the heavens:
> a time to be born and a time to die,
>   a time to plant and a time to uproot,
> a time to kill and a time to heal,
>   a time to tear down and a time to build,
> a time to weep and a time to laugh,
>   a time to mourn and a time to dance,
> a time to scatter stones and a time to gather them,
>   a time to embrace and a time to refrain from embracing,
> a time to search and a time to give up,
>   a time to keep and a time to throw away,

a time to tear and a time to mend,
   a time to be silent and a time to speak,
a time to love and a time to hate,
   a time for war and a time for peace.
What do workers gain from their toil? I have seen the burden
God has laid on the human race. He has made everything
beautiful in its time. He has also set eternity in the human
heart; yet no one can fathom what God has done from
beginning to end.

(Ecc 3:1-11)

The Hebrews were fond of the mysticism of numbers. There are 28
elements in this piece. The symbolism is built around the number 7 which
means fullness and the number 4 which represents the four cardinal points,
the fulness of space. For Qoheleth nobody can take from or add to the
number of days one has (3:14). For Qoheleth the flow of days is
incomprehensible. There is nothing there for one to focus on…

> "For the living know that they will die,
> but the dead know nothing;
> they have no further reward,
> and even their name is forgotten."

(Ecc 9:5)

He remarks whimsically "… a live dog is better off than a dead lion" (9:4).
He also says:

> "In this meaningless life of mine I have seen both of these:
> the righteous perishing in their righteousness,
> and the wicked living long in their wickedness."

(7:15)

He tells us

> "No one can comprehend what goes on under the sun. Despite
> all their efforts to search it out, no one can discover its
> meaning. Even if the wise claim they know, they cannot really
> comprehend it."

(8:17)

In chapter 6 he talks about how people enjoy wealth but when they die others enjoy it (6:1-3).

We see in this Qoheleth wrestling with time and its meaning. The passage 3:1-8 is in itself beautiful and is much quoted. Len Deighton, the author of spy thrillers, quotes it in his book 'Berlin Game'[1] Mikhail Gorbachev quoted Qoheleth when he met the bishop of Poitiers, J. Rozier and the French Dominican, J. Cardonnel. He greeted them with the words: "A time to scatter stones and a time to gather them" (Ecc 3:5). The Nicaraguan poet Rubén Darío (1867-1910) based his sonnet 'Gaita Galica' on Qo 3:1-8.

'Turn! Turn! Turn! (To everything there is a season)' is a song written by Pete Seeger in the 1950's based on Ecclesiastes 3:1-8. The song was originally released in 1962 as 'To Everything There is a Season' and then later on Seeger's own 'The Bitter and the Sweet'. The song became an international hit in 1965 when it was adapted by the American folk-rock group 'The Byrds'. The biblical text points to there being a time and place for all things: birth and death, killing and healing, sorrow and laughter, war and peace. "There is a time for every purpose under heaven" (Pete Seeger).

In Greek mythology at Plutonium in Phrygia the mouth of Hades was thought to be there because of the sulphurous fumes found there. The god Apollo had his own small temple there and one could read on the walls there: "There are times of life: When then are you so vainly anxious, o men." Qoheleth's meditation on time is in accord with thought in the Mediterranean basin at that time.

Qoheleth uses the Hebrew word 'zeman' which means season. He states "… a season (zeman) for every activity under the heavens" (3:1). It means the season in which we live. 'Zeman' (seasons) has different times (in Hebrew 'et'). The topic of time was a favourite one with Wisdom writers. In Sir 39:16-34 time marches onwards. As we saw Qoheleth questions the value of this march of time (e.g. P:15). The lists in Qoheleth are personal time but with cosmic significance. There is a "time to be born and a time to die." This is out of human times but the rest are under our control. In V3 the reference "a time to kill and a time to heal" seems to refer to society's reaction to transgressions. The time to die refers to capital punishment.

[1] Len Deighton, Berlin Game (London: 1983).

'The time to heal' refers to the work of physicians and other kinds of helpers to improve the life of an ailing person. At the time of Qoheleth sickness was regarded as a punishment from God and nothing could be done for the sick one. Qoheleth affirms the right of the physician to intervene and heal the sick. The Book of Job also questions whether sickness and misfortune are the results of personal sins. In the Gospel of John the disciples look at a man born blind and wonder what sin caused this. We read:

> As he went along, he saw a man blind from birth. His disciples asked him, "Rabbi, who sinned, this man or his parents, that he was born blind?"
>
> "Neither this man nor his parents sinned," said Jesus, "but this happened so that the works of God might be displayed in him. As long as it is day, we must do the works of him who sent me. Night is coming, when no one can work. While I am in the world, I am the light of the world."
>
> After saying this, he spit on the ground, made some mud with the saliva, and put it on the man's eyes. "Go," he told him, "wash in the Pool of Siloam" (this word means "Sent"). So the man went and washed, and came home seeing.
>
> (John 9:1-7)

There is a time to dance, a time to cast away stones. The poetic quality of the list shows the tragic quality of life can be artfully presented. The culminating verse 8 speaks of the human experience of love and hate, war and peace. Thus do peace and birth bracket the entire list. In this way death and war are demoted to realities that, though both profound and universal, have neither the first nor the last word.

This part 3:1-8 is beautiful but then we see Qoheleth's anguish break through. He asks: "What do workers gain from their toil? I have seen the burden God has laid upon the human race" (3:9f). All is vanity and chasing of the wind. We saw earlier how Qoheleth saw the futility of existence, including his own. Yet he can say: "He (God) has made everything beautiful in its time" (3:12). He oscillates between futility and hope. He prods us the reader to grapple with time, our time. Qoheleth's tragedy is not to find his own time and meaning. Perhaps in a tragic way this was actually his time. He had come to question the older wisdom he had received and the time has not yet come for new wisdom to take its place. This was Qoheleth's time – he was enabling new beginnings and a new wisdom.

T. S. Eliot wrote in the Four Quartets:

> In my beginning is my end. In succession
> Houses rise and fall, crumble, are extended,
> Are removed, destroyed, restored, or in their place
> Is an open field, or a factory, or a by-pass.
> Old stone to new building, old timber to new fires,
> Old fires to ashes, and ashes to the earth
> Which is already flesh, fur and faeces,
> Bone of man and beast, cornstalk and leaf.
> Houses live and die: there is a time for building
> And a time for living and for generation
> And a time for the wind to break the loosened pane
> And to shake the wainscot where the field-mouse trots
> And to shake the tattered arras woven with a silent motto.
>
> (East Coker)

Like Qoheleth he wonders at the passing of time. Unlike however Qoheleth and his own creation Prufrock he now sees things in the light of the death and resurrection of Jesus. The beginning, rooted in the first creation, provides the way for the grace and forgiveness in Jesus. This is the basis for our trust and hope. The way to hope comes by looking inward and realising we are all interconnected. 'East Coker' was meant as a message of hope to communities that would suffer World War II.

"In my beginning is my end": each stage leads on to another. This is reminiscent of Qoheleth. He concentrates on natural harmonies and harmony. Time here is linear unlike Qoheleth. Eliot tries to make the reader embrace paradox and avoid looking at a purely mechanistic view of the world: East Coker was where Eliot's namesake and distant ancestor Sir Thomas Elyot lived in the sixteenth century. It was this place that inspired Eliot to write "East Coker", the second of the 'Four Quartets'. My beginning leads me into the eternal moment.

Søren Aabye Kierkegaard

Kierkegaard (+1855) was a Danish philosopher and theologian who wrote during the nineteenth century. Often considered the Father of existential philosophy including Nietzsche and Jean-Paul Sartre. He was born in Copenhagen, Denmark, in 1813. Many of his siblings died young. He was surrounded by death. As a young man Søren Kierkegaard attended the University of Copenhagen. During this time Kierkegaard met a young woman named Regina Olsen. They were engaged to be married but Kierkegaard broke off the engagement with no explanation in 1841. Kierkegaard had become an author and was exploring themes like anxiety and despair, angst, and the meaning of our lives. His path was a lonely one. He explained the subjectivity of each one's experience. It is tempting to think that Kierkegaard knew his vocation was a lonely one and he did not wish to visit this loneliness on Regina Olsen. Towards the end of his life he had difficulty with the established church. He longed to put 'Christianity' into Christendom. He saw reality as absurd like Qoheleth and it was unexplainable. Kierkegaard believed that reason was insufficient to sort out the absurdity of human existence. In his later writings Kierkegaard entered a religious phase in his writings. He explored belief in God, Jesus Christ, and his idea that individuals should take a leap of faith for their spiritual development. In his book 'Fear and Trembling' (1843) he explores the biblical story of Abraham and the relationship between religion and ethics. Earlier I called Qoheleth as a Biblical Cezanne. He saw things differently from others and explored things from different viewpoints. I also see him as a Biblical Kierkegaard. Kierkegaard's nickname was the 'fork'. This was due to his eating habits as a child. It stuck because his writing was like a fork which prodded the reader to think. He used a variety of pseudonyms in his writing taking up different positions. The readers were left to work out for themselves what their own position was.

For Kierkegaard Christian faith calls us not to seek to hide ourselves from God. The definition of faith in "The Sickness unto Death"[2] is profound: "Faith is: that the self in being itself and in being willing to be itself rests transparently before God." When God is known through Christ, the self, however broken, can will to be itself because the self is accepted by God

---

[2] Søren Kierkegaard, The Sickness unto Death (London: 1989), p. 82. The original text was published in 1849.

and before God can take on the task of becoming the self god has called us to be in Him. A human self is something that one must become, not something that is by virtue of being born or that happens as a matter of course. Kierkegaard saw the human being as spirit. God is spirit and is independent of creation.

'The Sickness unto Death' begins with a response to a phrase in the Gospel of John 11:4: "This sickness is not unto death." According to Kierkegaard an individual is in despair if he does not align himself with God or with God's plan for the self. In this way he 'loses' himself. Human experience and human existence exists between "the finite and the infinite" and between "the possible and the necessary." We must become conscious that the source and ground of the "self" is love, "the power that creates it." When one fails to understand the true nature of the self or the true nature of the power that creates and sustains it one is in despair.

There are three kinds of despair presented in the book: One of them relates to being unconscious of having a self; another to not wanting to be oneself, and the third to feeling that one is not oneself. He describes the first as "unauthentic despair", because it is born of ignorance. In this state one is unaware that one has a self. The second kind of despair is the refusal to accept the self. This is the state in which one realises that one has a self, but avoids the responsibility to realise this. The third kind is awareness of the self without a willingness to acknowledge the dependance of that self on love. To not to be in despair means to have reconciled the finite with the infinite, to exist in awareness of one's own self and of living in love's gaze and power. People ascribe the name "God" to the "power that created" the self. Kierkegaard used the pseudonym "Anti-Climacus" in the writing of the book. Kierkegaard was exploring what it means to share a personal relationship with God and how God is love are the real subjects of the book. It is by prayer that we enter this world and see who we are. For a finite being to be spiritual one must go through a process of being, in which the individual and the individual's choices make a difference. "The eternal in a person can be demonstrated by the fact that despair cannot consume the self" (Sickness, p. 21). Blaise Pascal gives an account of what strange creatures we human beings are:

> "What kind of freak then is man? How novel, how monstrous,
> how chaotic, how paradoxical, how prodigious! Judge of all

things, feeble earthworm, repository of truth, sink of doubt and error, glory and refuse of the universe.[3]

Pascal (+1662) was a French mathematician, inventor, philosopher and writer. In his view of the chaotic nature of humanity he helps us accept the reality of our confused situation. He spoke of the "grandeur and misère" of the human situation. We care called to greatness but we fail and often fall short. This is why Kierkegaard's emphasis on love and his acceptance of us in our weakness is a source of strength. God's forgiveness is there for us. His mercy is greater than our weakness.

Kierkegaard did not believe there is such a thing as a common human nature, he does not think that a human being's personal identity is exhausted by the common human nature. Each person has a unique role to play in God's great economy. This is the answer to Qoheleth. Our time is God's time and we exist in him. God has given each one of us a specific individual mission. To use a metaphor Kierkegaard uses, each person has a unique divine name. Each of us has the task of "remembering" that name, of trying to decide what "calling" or "vocation" we have been given and whatever gifts and talents we have must be developed to fulfill that calling. He compares our giving ourselves over to God in this way: "Losing oneself in possibility may be compared with a child's utterance of vowel sounds" (p. 37). These are the first childlike steps we must take. "In order for a person to become aware of his self and God, imagination must raise him higher than the miasma of probability, it must teach him to hope and fear" (p. 41). We can do this because "for God everything is possible at every moment" (p. 39f). This is a faith that God will not allow a life to become wasted, regardless of what happens. He describes the person of faith:

> "The believer sees and understands his downfall, humanly speaking... but he believes. For this reason he does not collapse. He leaves it entirely to God how he is to be helped but he believes that for God everything is possible" (SUD, 39)

The person may believe in miracles but the true miracle consists in allowing him to come through what most people would describe as a catastrophe or great horror.

---

[3] Blaise Pascal, Pensées, trans. A. Krailsheimer (New York: 1966) p. 64.

The Concept of Anxiety (1844):

In Kierkegaard's time there was little emphasis on emotions. It would be Freud and Nietzsche who would again show the importance of emotions and passion. "We think with our bodies" said Nietzsche. Kierkegaard had this insight before this. He said truth exists for the particular individual only as "he himself produces it in action."[4]

"The Concept of Anxiety", published in 1844, is a book by Kierkegaard. He held that "anxiety is to be understood as orientated toward freedom" (p. 138). He defines freedom as possibility. The characteristic of being human lies in the range of our possibility. It is something we conceive of and by creative activity try to carry it into actuality. With this comes "anxiety." It comes with the possibility of freedom. The child learns to walk, and moves on to school and the adult moves into marriage and maybe a new job. Such possibilities are like roads ahead not yet traversed and experienced. This involves anxiety – "normal anxiety" and not "neurotic anxiety". "Neurotic anxiety" results from the individual's failure to move ahead with his life. There is an anxiety in not realising our potential. There is a fear that we are as nothing – the fear of being nothing. He says:

> "Possibility means I can. In a logical system it is convenient enough to say that possibility passes over into actuality. In reality it is not so easy, and an intermediate determinant is necessary. This intermediate determinant is anxiety…"
>
> (p. 44)

Kierkegaard looks at the development, as we saw, of the child. With this development comes "self-awareness". He looks at the story of Adam in Genesis. He sees Adam's "sin" as the individual's awakening into self-consciousness. With this conscious choice comes the source of the nature of possibility and of the possibilities that go with it. There grows the possibility of isolation and powerlessness and this produces anxiety. Becoming who we are involves confronting our anxiety. Kierkegaard speaks of the "alarming possibility of being able" (p. 40). To will to be oneself is our vocation. We are meant to be the people God has called us to be. In this is our freedom. We are called to be conscious of our world and

---

[4] Søren Kierkegaard, The Concept of Anxiety (New York: 2015), p. 123.

our place in it. "The more consciousness, the more self..." (Sickness Unto Death, p. 43). Kierkegaard's gift to modern psychotherapy is to show that selfhood depends upon the individual's capacity to confront anxiety and move ahead in spite of it. Freedom depends on how one relates to oneself in our everyday existence. This means that freedom depends on how responsibly and autonomously one relates to oneself. Self-awareness enables self-conscious historical development. We become ourselves in a certain historical time.

Anxiety can and often does involve an inner conflict. Anxiety can be fear yet it keeps a dialogue with its object, what it wants to be but it must confront the situation it is in (p. 92). Kierkegaard realises this can be difficult for us to read and hear. He goes on to say:

> "Anxiety is a desire for what one dreads, a sympathetic antipathy. Anxiety is an alien power which lays hold of an individual, and yet one cannot tear oneself away, nor has a will to do so; for one fears, but what one fears one desires. Anxiety then makes the individual impotent."

Our inner conflicts have been described by Freud, Horney and others. These fears can be seen in extreme forms in neurosis. Kierkegaard does not limit himself to neurotic phenomena. He believes in every possibility, in every experience of anxiety beyond infancy, there is a conflict present. As we grow and try to actualise our possibilities, we have to face the prospect of not doing so. We can arrive at a shutting down situation and we can sacrifice our freedom. In fear we can move away from the object feared whereas in anxiety there is a persistent inner conflict in operation and we can have an ambivalent attitude to the object. However once we can accept that the presence of anxiety means a conflict is going on, and as long as this is true, a constructive solution is possible.

Psalm 139:

This psalm is a form of the lament. The poor man puts his case before God. He remembers who God is: He recalls who he is before God and this is the reason for his hope. He says:

For you created my inmost being;
   you knit me together in my mother's womb.
I praise you because I am fearfully and wonderfully made;
   your works are wonderful,
   I know that full well.
My frame was not hidden from you
   when I was made in the secret place,
   when I was woven together in the depths of the earth.
Your eyes saw my unformed body;
   all the days ordained for me were written in your book
   before one of them came to be.

(Ps 139:13-16)

His faith in God is rooted in the fact that he is God's creation. He formed his innermost parts. The general theme is that of the development of the embryo or the development of the foetus in the womb. He is beautifully made. He thanks God for the wonder of his being. All of what God has called to be is good. God knows him through and through...

How precious to me are your thoughts, God!
   How vast is the sum of them!
Were I to count them,
   they would outnumber the grains of sand—
   when I awake, I am still with you.

(Ps 139:17-18)

The psalmist knows he is a thought of God. He knows he is loved. God's thoughts of the person are more than the grains of sand on the seashore. God's thoughts of us are even more than this. Whether the psalmist is asleep or awake he is close to God. He is more tender than a mother and cares for the psalmist more than a mother does for her child. God is closer to us than we are to ourselves. Thoughts of love are in God's very nature for us. By praying psalm 139 we open ourselves to realise this.

Chapter 6

From Self-Hatred to Acceptance

In the writings of Leonardo da Vinci he laments: "God, you who sell us many goods but at the cost of much struggle." This was written by a man who did much in science. Qoheleth lacks this faith in God and doesn't see any value in his work. In writing in the name of Solomon he has Solomon speak about what would happen to his work when he dies. His kingdom would be broken into two parts (1 Kings 12; 14; Sirach 47:23). All the work of Solomon would be hid in a nothingness. On one hand he sees the value of wisdom against stupidity but then he sees that this too is "vanity". This battle rages in the heart of Qoheleth. He says:

> Then I turned my thoughts to consider wisdom,
>   and also madness and folly.
> What more can the king's successor do
>   than what has already been done?
> I saw that wisdom is better than folly,
>   just as light is better than darkness.
> The wise have eyes in their heads,
>   while the fool walks in the darkness;
> but I came to realize
>   that the same fate overtakes them both.

> Then I said to myself,

> "The fate of the fool will overtake me also.
>   What then do I gain by being wise?"
> I said to myself,
>   "This too is meaningless."
> For the wise, like the fool, will not be long remembered;
>   the days have already come when both have been forgotten.
> Like the fool, the wise too must die!

Toil Is Meaningless

So I hated life, because the work that is done under the sun was grievous to me. All of it is meaningless, a chasing after the wind. I hated all the things I had toiled for under the sun, because I must leave them to the one who comes after me. And who knows whether that person will be wise or foolish? Yet they will have control over all the fruit of my toil into which I have poured my effort and skill under the sun. This too is meaningless. So my heart began to despair over all my toilsome labor under the sun. For a person may labor with wisdom, knowledge and skill, and then they must leave all they own to another who has not toiled for it. This too is meaningless and a great misfortune. What do people get for all the toil and anxious striving with which they labor under the sun? All their days their work is grief and pain; even at night their minds do not rest. This too is meaningless.

(Ecc 2:12-23)

In the face of death Qoheleth sees all as "vanity", "useless", "empty" ('hebel'). The destiny of the one who makes money still is to die. Qoheleth values wisdom (V13-14). It does not bring peace. In fact it is not even attainable fully (see 7:23-24). In vv14-17 fools are good as blind because they walk in darkness. But he interjects with the "yet". He sways back and forth between wisdom and being good and "yet" all is vanity. He admits he hates life.

In 2:20-23 he speaks of the absurdity of working hard and then leaving the fruits of one's labors to someone else. Literally translated the Hebrew of v.23 reads: "Even at night my heart, will not lie down." The heart is the centre of emotive life and intellectual life. It is the seat of emotions. Gaining wealth and then giving it to someone who wastes it is a reality.

Qoheleth sees the great pain that the attainment of wisdom means. The attainment of wisdom offers no guarantee of an enduring name. For Qoheleth knowledge brings the tragic vision that one is doomed to universal obliteration. Herman Melville, in his poem "A Spirit Appeared to Me" which takes its cue from these verses said:

A Spirit appeared to me, and said
"Where now would you choose to dwell?

In the Paradise of the Fool,
Or in wise Solomon's hell?"

Never he asked me twice:
"Give me the fool's Paradise."

For Qoheleth, who had no vision of a meaningful afterlife, death leveled the distinction between the wise and the foolish. If you are wise, then in the end it doesn't matter. "So I hated life" he exclaims. In chapter 4 Qoheleth we see more of his negativity. He says:

Again I looked and saw all the oppression that was taking place under the sun:

I saw the tears of the oppressed—
    and they have no comforter;
power was on the side of their oppressors—
    and they have no comforter.
And I declared that the dead,
    who had already died,
are happier than the living,
    who are still alive.

(Ecclesiastes 4:1-2)

In chapter 7 he continues the complaint of the verse, we read:

In this meaningless life of mine I have seen both of these:

the righteous perishing in their righteousness,
    and the wicked living long in their wickedness.

(Ecc 7:15)

Another translation of "meaningless" is "futile" (Berean Standard Bible). In the end this is how Qoheleth sees his life and efforts. Because of this he sees people negatively. He cries out:

"Look," says the Teacher, "this is what I have discovered:

"Adding one thing to another to discover the scheme of things—

> while I was still searching
>   but not finding—
> I found one upright man among a thousand,
>   but not one upright woman among them all.
> This only have I found:
>   God created mankind upright,
>   but they have gone in search of many schemes."

(Ecc 7:27-29)

One could translate 7:29 as saying that people tangled themselves up in many schemes and questions and went on to follow their own doomed path. He doesn't think he can ever find a good woman. He is not so hard on men (he being a man). He believes that maybe you can find one in a thousand. When we are all out of love with ourselves we do not see the good in others. When we feel we are of no value we carry that negativity into our view of others. Jim Morrison of The Doors put it this way:

> People are strange
> When you're a stranger
> Faces look ugly
> When you're alone
>
> Women seem wicked
> When you're unwanted
> Streets are uneven
> When you're down
>
> When you're strange
> Faces come out of the rain
> When you're strange
> No one remembers your name
> When you're strange
> When you're strange
> When you're strange
>
> People are strange
> When you're a stranger
> Faces look ugly
> When you're alone

(People Are Strange)

The Outcast:

"Fool's Overture" was released in 1977 on Supertramp's "Even in the Quietest Moments". The listener is treated with a collage of recording techniques and musical virtuosity. We hear Churchill's words about how: "we shall go to the end." In it Roger Hodgson reminisces how in the 1930's people ignored the warning from people like Churchill about the rise of Nazism to the cost of millions of lives.

Another voice trying to warn the world was Paul Tillich (+1965). He fled to America because he fell foul of the Nazi regime in the 1930's but when he spoke of the dangers of this regime he was ignored and laughed at. Qoheleth had warned us:

> There is an evil I have seen under the sun, the sort of error that arises from a ruler:
> Fools are put in many high positions, while the rich occupy the low ones.
> I have seen slaves on horseback, while princes go on foot like slaves.
> Whoever digs a pit may fall into it; whoever breaks through a wall may be bitten by a snake.
> Whoever quarries stones may be injured by them; whoever splits logs may be endangered by them.
> If the ax is dull and its edge unsharpened, more strength is needed but skill will bring success.
> If a snake bites before it is charmed, there is no profit for the charmer.
> Words from a wise man's mouth are gracious, but a fool is consumed by his own lips.
> At the beginning his words are folly; at the end they are wicked madness--
> and the fool multiplies words. No one knows what is coming-- who can tell him what will happen after him?
> A fool's work wearies him; he does not know the way to town.
> Woe to you, O land whose king was a servant and whose princes feast in the morning.

> (Ecc 10:5-16)

Here Qoheleth laments the unpredictability of life. Folly can manifest itself in hard-headedness which is a source of self-deception, that fatal inclination not to be distracted from action by the facts. Barbara Tuchman explores this theme in her book "The March of Folly: From Troy to Vietnam".[1] Rottenness is manifest in folly as it is in outright sin. One should not be surprised at the power of stupid people. A friend of mine called this: "The Power of STUPID!" They can insinuate themselves into the power structure of an organisation and find themselves in a position of power and influence. I had better stop there!

Paul Tillich (1886-1965) was born in the small village of Starzeddel which was part of Germany. He studied at several universities. In 1912 Tillich was ordained as a Lutheran minister in the Province of Brandenburg. He became a chaplain during World War I. There he saw the great suffering that "folly" inflicted on people. He had several nervous breakdowns during the war. He kept his sanity by reading Nietzsche and looking at books on beautiful paintings. After the war he taught in many universities. However, after the rise of Hitler things changed. He was dismissed from his position at university. Reinhold Niebuhr had known Tillich and invited him to teach at New York City Union Theological Seminary. He tried to warn the world of the menace of Hitler, but he was ignored. It was only after the war that he was appreciated. He was always an outsider.

One of his most famous works was "The Courage to Be".[2] He sees courage as being rooted in the structure of being. The courage to be is the ethical act in which man affirms his own being in spite of those elements of existence which conflict with his essential self-affirmation (p. 3). Courage involves striving towards "self-preservation or towards self-affirmation that makes a thing what it is" (p. 21). Even though life is ambiguous "courage is the power of life to affirm itself in spite of this ambiguity, while the negation of life because of its negativity is an expression of cowardice" (p. 27). The courage to be takes into itself the anxiety of death. He analyses anxiety in the next four chapters. He goes on to describe faith as the courage to accept acceptance. He sees despair and doubt as necessary tools of faith. The courage not to despair "takes despair into itself and resists the radical threat of nonbeing by the courage to be oneself" (p. 140). When one has the

[1] Barbara W. Tuchman, The March of Folly: From Troy to Vietnam (New York: 1984).

[2] Paul Tillich, The Courage to Be (New York: 2000, 1st ed. 1952).

courage to take the anxiety of meaninglessness upon oneself, a true power is revealed: "The courage to be is rooted in the God who appears when God has disappeared in the anxiety of doubt" (p. 190). Once a woman who suffered mentally came to Tillich, deeply disturbed. She told him she wrestled with her demons every day. Tillich told her he did the same every day. She was stunned at this response. She stopped pushing her thoughts away. She learned to accept them and she found peace. She felt accepted and this helped her.[3]

For Tillich it was when he came to God he had the feeling of total acceptance. He said that even in the face of despair...

> "There is a third element in absolute faith, the acceptance of being accepted. Of course, in the state of despair there is nobody and nothing that accepts. But there is the power of acceptance itself which is experienced. Meaninglessness, as long as it is experienced, includes an experience of the "power of acceptance." To accept this power of acceptance consciously is the religious answer of absolute faith, of faith which has been deprived by doubt of any concrete content, which nevertheless is faith and the source of the most paradoxical manifestation of the courage to be."
>
> (The Courage to Be, p. 175-177)

Tillich had experienced many negative things in his life. Yet in the face of this he still affirmed life. All the negative voices that afflicted him in his heartaches and disappointments were acknowledged, but he found his faith in the love and acceptance of God saw him through. This was his answer for those who felt fear, anxiety, doubt and meaninglessness. When we accept ourselves we can accept others.

A Sermon: Accept you are accepted:

In Tillich's book "The Shaking of the Foundations"[4] we have the sermons of Tillich. He gives in sermon form what he said in "The Courage to Be".

---

[3] This story was told by Tillich's friend Rollo May in Love and Will (New York: 1969), p. 145.

[4] Paul Tillich, The Shaking of the Foundations (New York: 2014). This is a collection of his sermons.

He begins by asking us what it means to be struck by grace. We cannot change our lives unless we allow them to be transformed by that stroke of grace. We may accept Scripture or teachings without any heart. Tillich tells us that God can come when we are in "great pain and restlessness." Life can be intolerable for us – then we have that moment when we feel a sudden peace. It is then we know that we are loved, we are accepted:

> "...when the old compulsions reign within us as they have for decades, when despair destroys all joy and courage. Sometimes at that moment a wave of light breaks into our darkness, and it is as though a voice were saying: "You are accepted. You are accepted, accepted by that which is greater than you, and the name of which you do not know. Do not ask for the name now; perhaps you will find it later. Do not try to do anything now; perhaps later you will do much. Do not seek for anything; do not perform anything; do not intend anything. Simply accept the fact that you are accepted!" If that happens to us, we experience grace. After such an experience we may not be better than before, and we may not believe more than before. But everything is transformed. In that moment, grace conquers sin, and reconciliation bridges the gulf of estrangement. And nothing is demanded of this experience, no religious or moral or intellectual presupposition, nothing but acceptance."

It means that we feel a sudden peace, what Tillich calls "acceptance". As "The Courage to Be" he tells us that we need courage. We can be overwhelmed by anxiety, despair or loneliness. To stay open in gentle prayer opens the door for us to feel the peace in the midst of our pain. Oscar Wilde said: "How else but through a broken heart may Lord Christ enter in?" This moment helps us cope with life.

Acceptance comes in the face of non-acceptance. So many experiences make us believe we are not accepted. We spend a lot of our time trying to prove we are worthy. It is easier than one thinks to hate oneself and this leads to mental illness. In the face of this it is hard to accept acceptance, but in accepting acceptance we are healed. God is love (1 Jn 4:8,16) and this is his nature. He loves totally; we don't and our experiences of love are flawed. Tillich point us to this love. It is there for us.

Leonard Cohen (+2016) was a Canadian singer-songwriter, poet and novelist. He explored many themes in his work. In his 1992 album, 'The Future' he recored the song 'Anthem.' In it he catches the themes we have been discussing:

> "Ring the bells that still can ring
> Forget your perfect offering
> There is a crack, a crack in everything
> That's how the light gets in."

Leonard Cohen didn't like explaining his music but he did make a statement about 'Anthem' on the 'The Future Radio Special', a special CD released by Sony in 1992. He said...

> "The future is no excuse for an abdication of your own personal responsibilities towards yourself and your job and your love. "Ring the bells that still can ring": they're few and far between but you can find them.
> This situation does not admit of solution of perfection. This is not the place where you make things perfect, neither in your marriage, nor in your work, nor anything, nor your love of God, nor your love of family or country. The thing is imperfect."

'Hallelujah' is another of Cohen's songs. it was originally recorded in 1984 on his album 'Various Positions (1984)'. It was not successful initially but John Cale recorded a version in 1991 which got notice. Cohen said: "the world is full of conflicts and full of things that cannot be reconciled. But there are moments when we reconcile and embrace the whole mess, and that's what I mean by 'Hallelujah!' " He sings of the broken 'Hallelujah'. All our 'hallelujahs' come from our brokenness. 'Hallelujah' means praise you Yahweh (using the shorter form 'jah').

> "I did my best, it wasn't much
> I couldn't feel, so I tried to touch
> I've told the truth, I didn't come to fool ya
> And even though it all went wrong
> I'll stand before the Lord of Song
> With nothing on my tongue but Hallelujah"

Sinéad O'Connor recorded her own broken Hallelujah in her version of psalm 33, just called 33. The words are:

"Sing oh you righteous to the Lord
It's right that the upright should acclaim Him
Sing to Jah with your guitar
Turn up yer bass amp
Whack it up all the way to 'save him'

By the word of Jah heaven was made
By the breath of his mouth all its hosts
He gathers up the oceans like a mound
And stores the deep
Stores the deep in vaults

Sing him a new song
Sing sweet with shouts of joy
For the word of Jah is right
And he sees what is right
And he loves what is right
And the earth is full of his care"

(33)

Chapter 7

A Broken Hallelujah

Miguel de Unamuno (+1936) was a Spanish essayist, novelist, poet, philosopher, professor of Greek and Classics and rector of the University of Salamanca. He entered the University of Madrid in 1880 where he received his doctorate. After this he became professor of Language and Literature at the University of Salamanca. In 1901 he became rector of the university but lost his job when he publicly espoused the Allied cause in World War I. His opposition to General Miguel Primo de Rivera's rule in Spain led to his exile to the Canary Islands, from which he escaped to France. When the dictatorship collapsed he returned to Salamanca. In October 1936 he denounced General Francisco Franco's Falangists. He was placed under house arrest. He died of a heart attack two months later.

One of his most famous books was "The Tragic Sense of Life" (1913).[1] He looks at what gives meaning to our life, our longing to understand the "wherefore" of our destiny and our "thirst for eternal life", which he states are fundamental desires we all share. To have awareness of these questions is to have a tragic sense of life as we struggle with these questions.

He says we are more a feeling creature than a rational one:

> "Perhaps that which differentiates [man] from other animals is feeling rather than reason. More often I have seen a cat reason than laugh or weep. Perhaps it weeps or laughs inwardly – but then perhaps, also inwardly, the crab resolves equations of the second degree."

Society only has importance in so much as it furthers the life of the individual. Abstract philosophy is senseless. If we have to understand a

---

[1] Miguel de Unamuno, The Tragic Sense of Life (e-option Kindle ed.: 2020).

philosopher we have to see them as people of flesh and blood. The starting point for all philosophy is our hunger "our longing not to die, the hunger for personal immortality". He says we are all longing for immortality whether we achieve it or not. "The existence of God is ... deduced from the [desire for the] immortality of the soul, and not the immortality of the soul from the existence of God." He views as "vain" attempts at pseudo-immortality that people try to attain through works of art, or writing or other projects. He looks at fear and doubt and the difficulties of belief in this world and others. He argues, Qoheleth-like, that we give meaning to life through how we live in our limited time on earth. Our arguments for the existence of God, the rational arguments, are attempts by rationalists to console themselves before their deep-seated, unconscious disappointment born of believing that beyond death is only eternal darkness. He himself reached a point of skepticism which he defines as occurring when reason conflicts with desire, in this case, with the desire for immortality.

> "Skepticism, uncertainty --- the position to which reason, by practicing its analysis upon itself, upon its own validity, at last arrives --- is the foundation upon which the heart's despair [about the desire for immortality] must build up its hope."

With this in mind he looks at the intersection of reason's conflicts with desire. He looks at the ideas of love, pity, faith, belief and charity.

For Unamuno "faith" means trust and confidence in God's authority and cannot be rationally explained. He tells us that the longing for immortality is what we must do, however rational or contra-rational this desire may seem to be. It is the necessary requirement to achieve immortal life. He says:

> "We must needs believe in the other life, in the eternal life beyond the grave, and in an individual and personal life, in a life in which each one of us may feel his consciousness and feel that it is united, without being confounded, with all other consciousnesses in the Supreme Consciousness, in

God; we must needs believe in that other life in order that we may live this life, an endure it, and give it meaning and finality. And we must needs believe in that other life, perhaps, in order that we may deserve it, in order that we may obtain it, for it may be that he neither deserve it nor will obtain it who does not passionately desire it above reason and, if need be, against reason.

And above all, we must feel and act as if an endless continuation of our earthly life awaited us after death; and if it be that nothingness is the fate that awaits us we must not … so act that it shall be a just fate."

Unamuno throws light on Qoheleth. He struggles with faith and doubt, but for Qoheleth, he doesn't see or believe in an afterlife. "All is vanity and chasing of the wind." Our effort fades and is forgotten. He says:

I also said to myself, "As for humans, God tests them so that they may see that they are like the animals. Surely the fate of human beings is like that of the animals; the same fate awaits them both: As one dies, so dies the other. All have the same breath; humans have no advantage over animals. Everything is meaningless. All go to the same place; all come from dust, and to dust all return. Who knows if the human spirit rises upward and if the spirit of the animal goes down into the earth?"

(Ecc 3:18-21)

The term sons of man refers to humanity. The fate of human beings and animals is the same. As one dies so does the other. This is the nightmare of Unamuno that we have no life after death.

Ecclesiastes said that God "has placed eternity in our hearts" (3:11). We don't want things to just end. Yet we are like the beasts. Although it appears that we are smarter, have vision and have more authority yet the reality is that all is "hebel", vanity (see 1:2). We all go to the same place in the end. Emptiness is all.

In chapter 4 Qoheleth says:

> Again I looked and saw all the oppression that was taking
> place under the sun:
>
> I saw the tears of the oppressed —
>   and they have no comforter;
> power was on the side of their oppressors —
>   and they have no comforter.
> And I declared that the dead,
>   who had already died,
> are happier than the living,
>   who are still alive.
> But better than both
>   is the one who has never been born,
> who has not seen the evil
>   that is done under the sun.
>
> (Ecc 4:1-3)

He had finished chapter 3 with the hope that God will judge the wicked,
but now he looks at things again. The nature of oppression is a lack of
care for others. When oppressors use their power, influence or wealth or
position to oppress, it is logical to conclude that they will not bring
comfort. The idea of sighing has a ring of vapour ('*hebel*'). "Better off
is the one who never existed." The one who never existed knows
nothing of the fate of the oppressed. Mankind is destined to struggle
with evil activity. One thinks here of the works of Kafka (+1924). In
1914 he began to write his novel "The Trial" (Der Process) the story of
a man arrested and prosecuted by a remote, inaccessible authority, with
the nature of the crime revealed neither to him or to the reader. He tries
to deal with the absurdity of the situation. We are all locked in a prison
from which we cannot escape.

In the Bible God is seen as being on the side of the oppressed, the
individual or the nation (e.g. see Ps 71:21, 86:17; Is 40:1; Sam 1:1-2).
For Qoheleth God is deaf to the cry of the poor. The vision of God in the
Book of Proverbs is different: "The one who offends the poor one

offends the Creator" (Prov 14:31). In the face of these contradictions Qoheleth asks how can we love life?

Qoheleth's questioning expresses our deepest fears. Yet it is only in facing our fears and doubts that our faith can emerge in a new way. We are a broken people with many fears. Yet we can pray and raise up to God a "broken Hallelujah". Hallelujah means praise God – using the name 'Yah', a shorter form of Yahweh.

A Broken Hallelujah (Leonard Cohen)

Leonard Cohen (+2016) was a Canadian singer-songwriter, writer, poet and novelist. Themes that run throughout his work are faith and mortality, isolation and depression, betrayal and redemption, social and political conflict, sexual and romantic love, desire, regret and loss.

Cohen began a career as a poet and novelist during the 1950's and early 1960's and did not begin his musical career until 1967. His first album was "Songs of Leonard Cohen" (1967). This was followed by three more albums of folk music: "Songs for a Room" (1969), "Songs of Love and Hate" (1971) and "New Skin for the Old Ceremony" (1974). His next album "Death of a Ladies' Man" (1977) was a departure from his previous minimalist style. Jennifer Warnes describes Cohen's lyrics as follows:

> "Leonard acknowledges that the whole act of living contains immense amounts of sorrow and hopelessness and despair; and also passion, high hopes, deep love, and eternal love."
>
> (America Sings [Nov 11, 2016], Jennifer Warnes
> discusses Leonard Cohen, see YouTube)

Jennifer Warnes toured with Cohen as a backup singer, and she became a fixture on Cohen's albums, receiving all co-vocal credits on the 1984 album "Various Positions". 'Hallelujah' was released on this album in 1984. He sang it during his European tour in 1985. The song initially had little success but found greater popularity through a 1991 cover by John Cale (that was featured in the 2001 animated film 'Shrek'). Cale's version formed the basis for a later cover version by Jeff Buckley.[2] Janet Maslin in The New York Times Book Review said that Cohen spent years struggling with the song, which eventually became "one of the most haunting, inimitable and oft-performed songs in American musical history" (July 9, 2022). The term "Hallelujah" is used as an expression of gratitude to God. The ten is used 24 times in the Hebrew Bible (in the Book of Psalms), twice in deuterocanonical books and four times in the Book of Revelation. The phrase is used in Judaism as part of the Hallel prayers and it is also used in Christian prayer.

Cohen said of his song:

> "This world is full of conflicts and full of things that cannot be reconciled. But there are moments when we can reconcile and embrace the whole mess, and that's what I mean by 'Hallelujah'.[3]

Canadian singer K. D. Lang said she considered the song to be about "the struggle between having human desire and searching for spiritual wisdom. It's being caught between these two places" (David Friend [14 November 2016] in the Hamilton Spectator). Cohen said it was written to affirm his faith in life, not in some formal religious way, but with enthusiasm, with emotion.

> "I did my best, it wasn't much
> I couldn't feel, so I tried to touch
> I've told the truth, I didn't come to fool you
> And even though it all went wrong
> I'll stand before the Lord of Song
> With nothing on my tongue but Hallelujah

---

[2] The song is the subject of a 2012 book "The Holy or the Broken" by Alan Light and a 2022 documentary "Hallelujah: Leonard Cohen, A Journey, A Song" by Dan Geller and Dayna Goldfine.

[3] Ashley Fettes (4 December 20120 "How Leonard Cohen's Hallelujah Became Everybody's Hallelujah, The Atlantic.

Hallelujah, Hallelujah
Hallelujah, Hallelujah

Hallelujah, Hallelujah
Hallelujah, Hallelujah"

He expresses the loneliness of his struggle. Even though things went wrong he still comes before the mercy of God which is greater. In all the experiences of his life he cries "hallelujah" – his "broken hallelujah". It is easier than one thinks to hate oneself. To accept and love oneself as we are is a great grace. Cohen helps us do this through the music of "Hallelujah". We are broken and sinful but we trust more in God than in ourselves. It leads us to prayer. It is in prayer that we place ourselves before the Word of God. We find this word in sacred scripture and in the Word made flesh, Jesus (Jn 1:14). The Word of God is love for us. In placing ourselves before love we receive healing and forgiveness. We learn to love and in loving we grow more in love. Prayer is a loving dialogue with one whom we know loves us (St. Teresa of Avila). We can begin to experience this love in listening to "Hallelujah" and come to accept we are accepted.

In his song "Anthem" from the 1992 album "The Future" he said:

"Ring the bells that still can ring
Forget your perfect offering
There is a crack, a crack in everything
That's how the light gets in "

The 'cracks' our failures are the very place we meet God. It is there the light comes in. There is hope in darkness. As the psalm says

"Why are you cast down, my soul,
Why groan within me?
Hope in God; I will praise him still,
my saviour and my God."

(Ps 42:11)

In the Gospel of John, Jesus reassures us:

> "Do not let your hearts be troubled. You believe in God; believe also in me. My Father's house has many rooms; if that were not so, would I have told you that I am going there to prepare a place for you? And if I go and prepare a place for you, I will come back and take you to be with me that you also may be where I am."
>
> (Jn 14:1-3)

These words are meant for us when we are laid down with doubt and sadness.

In a book of poetry written after the album "Death of a Ladies' Man":

> "Everyone I know has died off
> except Leonard
> He can still be seen
> hobbling with his love"[4]

He died hobbling in life. All was a struggle. Cohen was ultimately the poet of loneliness. In his 1989 poetry collection, "Book of Mercy", he wrote: "Blessed are you who has given each man a shield of loneliness so that he cannot forget you. You are the truth of loneliness, and only your name addresses it. Strengthen my loneliness that I may be healed in your name, which is beyond all consolations that are uttered on this earth. Only in your name can I stand in the rush of time, only when this loneliness is yours can I lift my sins toward your mercy."[5] "In all our afflictions he was afflicted" (Isa 63:9). Our pain is God's pain. Jesus shows us this. He is with us in all our agony and it is this that gives us confidence in his love and mercy. God, then, is the loneliest of us all. Yet he never ceases to give the gift of life to us even when we feel far from him. This is why we can sing "Hallelujah".

---

[4] Leonard Cohen, "Final Examination" in Death of a Ladies' Man (Toronto: 1978), p. 212.
[5] Leonard Cohen, "Blessed Are You" in Book of Mercy (Toronto: 1984), p. 9.

Cohen began the song with a reference to King David. In the Middle Ages King David was believed to be the author of the Psalms. This position is no longer held. The psalms were the hymnbook of the Hebrew Bible. In the Book of Chronicles we hear of the singing of "joyous songs" (1 Chronicles 15:16). In "Hallelujah" Cohen refers to David's adulterous relationship with Bathsheba (2 Sam 11-12:25). He arranges for Uriah the Hittite to be killed in battle. He was Bathsheba's husband.

Cohen begins "Hallelujah" in the following manner:

"Now I've heard there was a secret chord
That David played, and it pleased the Lord
But you don't really care for music, do you?
It goes like this, the fourth, the fifth
The minor falls, the major lifts
The baffled king composing Hallelujah

Hallelujah, Hallelujah
Hallelujah, Hallelujah

Your faith was strong but you needed proof
You saw her bathing on the roof
Her beauty and the moonlight overthrew you
She tied you to a kitchen chair
She broke your throne, and she cut your hair
And from your lips she drew the Hallelujah

Hallelujah, Hallelujah
Hallelujah, Hallelujah"

David becomes a baffled king composing his "Hallelujah". He has sinned and now he places his trust in the mercy of God. He has to begin again. Cohen reflects on this. He too wants to come to God. He says:

"But it's not a crime that you're hear tonight
It's not some pilgrim who claims to have seen the Light
No, it's a cold and it's a very broken Hallelujah

Hallelujah, Hallelujah
Hallelujah, Hallelujah
Instrumental

Hallelujah, Hallelujah
Hallelujah, Hallelujah"

He doesn't come with a great crime. He is full of fear and doubt and hurt. He is lonely. He feels broken and he says of his Hallelujah it's a "cold and it's a very broken Hallelujah". We can be broken by life but even in the darkness we can still offer a broken "Hallelujah".

Crying Out to God That He May Hear Me

In Ps 63 the psalmist says "You are my God". The opposite side of the coin is Isa 43:1 where God addresses a despondent people and says, "You are mine". The psalmist is like one who is thirsty and exhausted after crossing an arid desert. He desperately longs to quench his thirst. His thirst is for God, to know him and be filled with his love. The psalm is used in public worship but it draws out what is latent in the human spirit. We all long for the peace of knowing God and feeling his love poured into our hearts.

As we read on the psalmist says: "my soul is satisfied". In faith he called out and he expresses his belief his cry is heard. That is why he sings for joy. The psalm is a form of sacrament. We express in words what we desire. It is here we meet God through the words and we live in faith that our cry is heard. He says: "my soul clings to you; your right hand holds me fast."

> "O God, you are my God, for you I long;
>   for you my soul is thirsting.
> My body pines for you
>   like a dry, weary land without water.
> So I gaze on you in the sanctuary
>   to see your strength and your glory.

For your love is better than life,
  my lips will speak your praise.
So I will bless you all my life,
  in your name I will lift up my hands.
My soul shall be filled as with a banquet,
  my mouth shall praise you with joy.

On my bed I remember you.
  On you I muse through the night
for you have been my help;
  in the shadow of your wings I rejoice.
My soul clings to you;
  your right hand holds me fast."

Chapter 8

Gimme Shelter

Shelter is one of our basic needs as human beings. It can mean a refuge from danger, a haven from worry, a comforting oasis in a desert of distress. "Gimme Shelter" is a song by The Rolling Stones and was released in 1969. It was on the album "Let it Bleed". Keith Richards spoke about the composition of the song:

> "I had been sitting by the window of my friend Robert Fraser's apartment on Mount Street in London with an acoustic guitar when suddenly the sky went completely black and an incredible monsoon came down. It was just people running about looking for shelter – that was the germ of the idea [for 'Gimme Shelter']," Richards told Harper's Bazaar. "We went further into it until it became, you know, rape and murder are 'just a shot away.'"

The lyrics of "Gimme Shelter" convey a bleak outlook on the world:

> "Ooh, see the fire is sweepin'
> Our streets today
> Burns like a red coal carpet
> Mad bull lost its way
>
> War, children
> It's just a shot away
>
> Rape, murder, it's just a shot away
> It's just a shot away"

It was the time of the Vietnam War. 1968 had seen the murders of Martin Luther King and Robert Kennedy. It was the time of the invasion of Czechoslovakia and the end of the Prague Spring. There were race riots in America. The Civil Rights movement in Ireland was becoming more violent. Terrorism was on the increase across Europe. There was a lot of hatred and fear in the air. Mick Jagger said "[Gimme Shelter] is a kind of end-of-the-world song really. It's apocalypse, the whole record's like that."

The atmosphere of the song is heightened by the vocals of Gospel singer Merry Clayton. Her emotive, near screeching vocals added a layer to the track that the Stones couldn't provide themselves.

Through the bleakness and darkness of "Shelter" there is still hope. Love is still possible...

> "I tell you love, sister
> It's just a kiss away"

"Shelter" is at once frightening but ultimately hopeful. Can we survive?

Their 1965 song "Satisfaction" caught the dissatisfaction of a generation. "Shelter" catches the same generation when a lot of illusions had been shattered and the optimism of the early 1960's had evaporated.

Qoheleth had experienced many changes in his lifetime. The things he had loved were no more. The Wisdom he studied had disappointed him. He is world-weary. He says:

> "So I reflected on all this and concluded that the righteous and the wise and what they do are in God's hands, but no one knows whether love or hate awaits them. All share a common destiny—the righteous and the wicked, the good and the bad, the clean and the unclean, those who offer sacrifices and those who do not.
>
> As it is with the good,
>   so with the sinful;
> as it is with those who take oaths,
>   so with those who are afraid to take them.

This is the evil in everything that happens under the sun:
The same destiny overtakes all. The hearts of people,
moreover, are full of evil and there is madness in their
hearts while they live, and afterward they join the dead."

(Ecclesiastes 9:1-3)

He too finds the world to be a place of fear and anxiety. He had believed
that the good and wise ones would be protected, but they are not. Again
all is 'absurd', 'empty', 'hebel'. Death and violence never have enough.

> "The leech has two daughters.
>   'Give! Give!' they cry.
> "There are three things that are never satisfied,
>   four that never say, 'Enough!'":
> the grave, the barren womb,
>   land, which is never satisfied with water,
>   and fire, which never says, 'Enough!'

(Prov 30:15-16)

Qoheleth goes on to speak of 'Sheol' in v4-5, a shady place where the
dead go. In the prophet Isaiah, Hezekiah the king, who is gravely ill,
describes Sheol:

> For the grave cannot praise you,
>   death cannot sing your praise;
> those who go down to the pit
>   cannot hope for your faithfulness.
> The living, the living—they praise you,
>   as I am doing today;
> parents tell their children
>   about your faithfulness.

(Isa 38:18-19)

Later in chapter 9 Qoheleth says:

> I have seen something else under the sun:
>
> The race is not to the swift
>   or the battle to the strong,

nor does food come to the wise
   or wealth to the brilliant
   or favour to the learned;
but time and chance happen to them all.
Moreover, no one knows when their hour will come:

As fish are caught in a cruel net,
   or birds are taken in a snare,
so people are trapped by evil times
   that fall unexpectedly upon them.
  (Ecc 9:11-12)

We are not in charge of our own destiny. Destiny and fate can overtake us. War, rape and violence of "Shelter" can destroy the good as well as the bad. We can rebel but to no avail. He uses an image from hunting and fishing to show how we are trapped. This is a common theme (see Ps 9:16-17; 10:10; 35:7; 57:7; 140:6; 141:10). There are times when we feel the onset of darkness and feel lost, lonely and confused. We cry "Gimme Shelter".

In 1967 The Doors recorded "The End". They catch the mood of what we have been talking about. We hear the words...

This is the end, beautiful friend
This is the end, my only friend
The end of our elaborate plans
The end of everything that stands

The end
No safety or surprise
The end
I'll never look into your eyes again

Can you picture what will be?
So limitless and free
Desperately in need of some stranger's hand
In a desperate land

Lost in a Roman wilderness of pain
And all the children are insane
All the children are insane
Waiting for the summer rain

Jim Morrison, the lead singer of 'The Doors' spoke of the pain of existing, of being human. He said of his song "The End" –

"Sometimes the pain is too much to examine, or even tolerate ... That doesn't make it evil, though – or necessarily dangerous. But people fear death even more than pain. It's strange that they fear death. Life hurts a lot more than death. At the point of death, the pain is over. Yeah – I guess it is a friend."[1]

"The End" was used in the Francis Ford Coppola film 'Apocalypse Now'.

The Apocalypse

The 'Book of the Apocalypse' is the final book of the New Testament. 'Apocalypse' means revelation. It is full of colourful and grotesque images. Seán Cassin who worked with drug addicts told me how those images spoke to the addicts who knew a world of fear and danger. The images spoke to their fears. When it came to liturgies those struggling quite often picked readings from 'The Apocalypse' to speak of their struggles. The Book consists of visions of John on the Island of Patmos in the Aegean Sea. He was exiled there because he "proclaimed God's word and gave testimony to Jesus" (Rev 1:9). It was written after the Roman armies had destroyed the Temple in Jerusalem and Jerusalem itself (see 2 Esdras 3:1-2; 28-31; Apocalypse of Baruch 10:1-3, 11:1; Sibylline Oracles 5:143, 159). he uses the term 'Babylon' to refer to Rome. The Babylonians in their time had destroyed the Temple.

[1] Lizzie James, Jim Morrison: Ten Years Gone (Creem Magazine, archived November 8, 2012).

In the Apocalyptic Books the seer is the recipient of visions and records them in writing. It contains secrets about the future. The original Apocalyptic literature had its origin in the Wisdom literature – Qoheleth belongs to this. In the Book of Revelation the seer John brought consolation in the midst of suffering when the people thought that God had abandoned them. This is true of all Apocalyptic literature. Ecclesiastes and other writers in Wisdom literature were concerned about universal truth, the meaning of life and death and what constitutes human good. Apocalyptica shows God is in charge and will ultimately triumph. In the Book of the Apocalypse of the New Testament the author describes a collection of visions, some of which are in the Heavenly realm and others on earth; some relating to the believing community as it anticipates persecution and others relating to those who have experienced suffering. G. K. Chesterton said that there are many strange animals and beasts in the Apocalypse but none as strange as those who try to interpret it! All these events find their meaning in the last chapter.

In chapter 19 we find the souls of the just gathered around God and his and his mercy seat We read:

> After this I heard what sounded like the roar of a great
> multitude in heaven shouting:
>
> "Hallelujah!
> Salvation and glory and power belong to our God,
> for true and just are his judgments.
> He has condemned the great prostitute
>   who corrupted the earth by her adulteries.
> He has avenged on her the blood of his servants."
> And again they shouted:
>
> "Hallelujah!
> The smoke from her goes up for ever and ever."
> The twenty-four elders and the four living creatures fell
> down and worshiped God, who was seated on the throne.
> And they cried:

"Amen, Hallelujah!"
Then a voice came from the throne, saying:

"Praise our God,
    all you his servants,
you who fear him,
    both great and small!"
Then I heard what sounded like a great multitude, like the
roar of rushing waters and like loud peals of thunder,
shouting:

"Hallelujah!
    For our Lord God Almighty reigns.
Let us rejoice and be glad
    and give him glory!
For the wedding of the Lamb has come,
    and his bride has made herself ready.
Fine linen, bright and clean,
    was given her to wear."
(Fine linen stands for the righteous acts of God's holy
people.)

(Rev 19:1-8)

A voice from the throne calls everyone to praise God – 'hallelujah' or
Alleluia (19:5) and the multitude responds with a sound so deafening
that it resembles water or thunder (19:6). The bride of the Lamb is
wearing costly garments. The bride is the church in its glorified state.
The garment is made up of the righteous deeds of the Holy ones (19:8;
cf 15:6). The work we do here on earth is not lost. It is used by God to
heal a broken world and leads to the creation of a new Heaven and new
Earth where there is peace. At the beginning of the Book the angel spoke
to the churches. Then we had the series of visions. What John is
communicating is that the daily ordinary life of the churches and the
people in them form part of God's plan for the healing and restoration
of all. We are not isolated individuals but are a part of humanity. We
pray that all people be saved (1 Tim 2:4). Jesus accomplished our
salvation on Calvary but he called us to play our part in healing and

saving the world. He is the vine and we are the branches (Jn 15:5). We share in his mission to heal the world and bring all people to rest in him. Each of us has a part to play given to us by God. We are all called to form the 'wedding garment of the bride' in 19:8. We so often fail to see the dignity of our calling. The world as seen by "Shelter", Qoheleth and "The End" is for all that not the end. Living our lives in faith brings healing in ways we do not understand. We place ourselves before the Word and allow the love expressed there to enter our lives. We are called to live in that love even in the face of the deepest darkness. St. Francis said "All the darkness in the world cannot extinguish the light of a single candle". No darkness can dispel even the tiniest light. In God's hands this light eventually will overcome all darkness. Jesus is the light of the world (Jn 8:12).

In chapter 21 we see the new Heaven and the new Earth. This healed world comes from the old Heaven and Earth. God has included us in the creation of the new Heaven and Earth. We read:

> Then I saw "a new heaven and a new earth," for the first heaven and the first earth had passed away, and there was no longer any sea. I saw the Holy City, the new Jerusalem, coming down out of heaven from God, prepared as a bride beautifully dressed for her husband. And I heard a loud voice from the throne saying, "Look! God's dwelling place is now among the people, and he will dwell with them. They will be his people, and God himself will be with them and be their God. 'He will wipe every tear from their eyes. There will be no more death' or mourning or crying or pain, for the old order of things has passed away."
>
> He who was seated on the throne said, "I am making everything new!" Then he said, "Write this down, for these words are trustworthy and true."
>
> (Rev 21:1-5)

Isaiah 65:17 had spoken of a new Heaven and a new Earth. Now we see it is coming to be. In the preceding vision John had recounted a scene in which the palette of God's creation had been made clean. Now from this comes the new Heaven and new Earth (21:1-2). The image of a bride had been used by Isaiah to describe how the exiles came home from the Babylonian exile.

> Lift up your eyes and look around;
>   all your children gather and come to you.
> As surely as I live," declares the Lord,
>   "you will wear them all as ornaments;
>   you will put them on, like a bride.
>
> (Isa 49:18)

This is God's dwelling and in Him we find our peace. There is no more pain, no more sadness. Every tear will be wiped away. This is our hope. God brings life out of the sadness of this world. We are all valuable in his sight. The prophet Ezekiel had promised this presence of God when he writes of God's word: "My dwelling shall be with them; I will be their God and they shall be my people" (Ezek 37:27). The old order denoted by the dragon, the beasts of the land and sea, Death, have all passed away. There is no suffering or death in the new order. Isaiah had spoken of this order. He quotes God's words "On this mountain the Lord God will wipe away the tears from all faces" (Isa 25:7-8). This is now accomplished. In Isaiah 55 we read:

> "Come, all you who are thirsty,
>   come to the waters;
> and you who have no money,
>   come, buy and eat!
> Come, buy wine and milk
>   without money and without cost.
> Why spend money on what is not bread,
>   and your labor on what does not satisfy?
> Listen, listen to me, and eat what is good,
>   and you will delight in the richest of fare.
> Give ear and come to me;
>   listen, that you may live.

I will make an everlasting covenant with you,
  my faithful love promised to David.

(Isa 55:1-3)

We are called to share this joy. This is our hope. It gives us courage to face the darkness and reassures us of God's final victory. Jesus conquered sin and death in his death and resurrection. He has called us to follow him and he has given us a place in his mission to bring about the new Heaven and Earth. We become a new creation "in Christ". In our broken 'hallelujah' he has heard our cry and leads us to life eternal. He calls us to help one another on the way.

Shelter from the Storm:

Bob Dylan recorded this song in 1974 and it was included on the album "Blood on the Tracks". In it he seeks to find salvation through love. The song opens with symbolism which can speak to a Christian...

> "'Twas in another lifetime, one of toil and blood
> When blackness was a virtue, the road was full of mud
> I came in from the wilderness, a creature void of form
> Come in, she said, 'I'll give you shelter from the storm'"

It is love that gives us shelter in the storm. God is the one who loves us. In Jesus we see and hear his Word make flesh (Jn 1:14). His word is love. It is in prayer and silence that we place ourselves before this and allow it to enter our hearts. All our loves are taken up into this love and we feel the love of God poured into our hearts by the Holy Spirit given us (Rom 5:5). In prayer the essential thing for us is to hear God's word and discern how to respond to him. God's word is himself sent into the world to heal it and bring it back to him. God speaks of his word made flesh: "This is my beloved Son; listen to him" (Mt 17:5). Harassed by life, exhausted, we look about for shelter. It is by surrender to God's love that we find this place of shelter. Ps 62 puts it this way:

Truly my soul finds rest in God;
    my salvation comes from him.
Truly he is my rock and my salvation;
    he is my fortress, I will never be shaken.
    (Ps 62:1)

Conclusion

Every Grain of Sand

At the end of chapter 11 the preacher Qoheleth urges people to live as
best they can while still alive (11:7). This has been a common theme as
we saw (cf 2:3, 24; 3:12, 27; 5:18; 8:15). Rejoice during a day of light,
but always remember the darkness is coming. One calls to mind Isaiah
14:11, 14, 16: "My child, treat yourself well, according to your means /
and present worthy offerings to the Lord... Do not deprive yourself of a
days enjoyment / do not let your share of desired good pass by you ...
Give and take and indulge yourself / because in Hades one cannot look
for luxury."

This leads us to the final words of Qoheleth. He says:

> Remember your Creator
>   in the days of your youth,
> before the days of trouble come
>   and the years approach when you will say,
>   "I find no pleasure in them"—
> 2 before the sun and the light
>   and the moon and the stars grow dark,
>   and the clouds return after the rain;
> 3 when the keepers of the house tremble,
>   and the strong men stoop,
> when the grinders cease because they are few,
>   and those looking through the windows grow dim;
> 4 when the doors to the street are closed
>   and the sound of grinding fades;
> when people rise up at the sound of birds,
>   but all their songs grow faint;
> 5 when people are afraid of heights
>   and of dangers in the streets;
> when the almond tree blossoms

and the grasshopper drags itself along
and desire no longer is stirred.
Then people go to their eternal home
and mourners go about the streets.
6 Remember him—before the silver cord is severed,
and the golden bowl is broken;
before the pitcher is shattered at the spring,
and the wheel broken at the well,
7 and the dust returns to the ground it came from,
and the spirit returns to God who gave it.
8 "Meaningless! Meaningless!" says the Teacher.
"Everything is Meaningless!"

(Ecc 12:1-8)

The set of images show us decay. Qoheleth adjures the young to remember their creator. He has no illusions about old age. There are days of trouble, the days of joylessness. The sun and the other heavenly bodes are not really darkened but the person who looks on and is old finds his sight failing. Those who work can no longer work. He uses the metaphor of the storm too where the house shakes, work ceases and darkness settles in. He uses the image of the lattices where the women look out at the decaying scene.

He centres in v.4-5 he uses images of "the doors to the street", "the sound of grinding" and he goes on to speak of the inability to sleep in the morning. These can refer to the deterioration of the body. We have the tragic picture of the old person whose body has failed in many respects. The picture turns at the end of v.5 to the funeral itself (see Job 3:6). The mourners are those professional wailers who could be hired to provide a suitable lamentation for the dead. This was a common feature of funerals in Ireland up to recent times.

In v6-7 he speaks of the silver cord, the golden bowl, a pitcher, fountain, wheel and cistern all refer to the failure of a single well. The sense of the passage is clear. He is telling the young person to live in the present and enjoy it because the precious water of life becomes unobtainable, and in a clear allusion to Gen 3:19, the dust returns to the earth... and the breath returns to God who gave it (v.7). The breath, for Qoheleth, means the life force that came from God in the first place (see Gen 2:7; see also Job 34:14-15; Ps 104:29).

The final verse 8 is similar to the opening thematic statement of the book (1:2) – "Vanity of vanities, says the Teacher, vanity of vanities! All is vanity." V8 reads "Vanity of vanities" says the Teacher "all is vanity." Here we see that Qoheleth did not believe in immortality.

Edgar Allan Poe refers to this part of Qoheleth in his poem "Lenore":

"Ah broken is the golden bowl! the spirit flown forever!
Let the bell toll!–a saintly soul floats on the Stygian river"

The text refers to the loss of life itself. As far as decline of individual life one can say: "I have no pleasure in them." Qoheleth tells us: "Banish anxiety from your mind, and put away pain from your body (11:10). He is thinking about the brevity of life. In an entirely different way Jesus tells us: "And can any one of you by worrying add a single hour to your span of life? And why do you worry about clothing? Consider the lilies of the field, how they grow; they neither toil nor spin, yet I tell you, even Solomon in all his glory was not clothed like one of these" (Matt 6:27-29). This is an invitation to a full life of trust, gratitude and courage not driven by a melancholy sense of the fleetingness of it all, but by the nearness of the kingdom of God and his righteousness (Matt 6:33).

Jesus also has Qoheleth-like realism when he says: "today's trouble is enough for today" (Matt 6:34). He goes on to tell his followers to be merciful, to make peace, to comfort those who mourn and to live life fully. Living this way is a foretaste of the kingdom of God even now. We can live life this way before "the golden bowl is broken, and the pitcher is broken at the fountain and the wheel is broken at the cistern" (Ecc 12:6). This concludes the teaching of Qoheleth.

You are Precious:

In Matthew 10:29-31 we read:

> "Are not two sparrows sold for a penny? Yet not one of them will fall to the ground outside your Father's care. And even the very hairs of your head are all numbered. So don't be afraid; you are worth more than many sparrows."

Here Jesus teaches us about how important we are to God. In Isaiah 43:4 we read: "You are precious in my eyes and honoured, and I love you." We are not used to thinking of ourselves in this way. Yet that is what we are.

Bob Dylan is an American singer-songwriter and Nobel Laureate in literature, 2016. His original name is Robert Zimmerman and he was born in Duluth, Minnesota in 1941. He was part of the protest movement in the early 1960's. "Every Grain of Sand" is a song written by Bob Dylan in the Spring of 1981 and released in August that year on Dylan's album 'Shot of Love'. It begins:

> "In the time of my confession, in the hour of my deepest need
> When the pool of tears beneath my feet flood every newborn seed
> There's a dyin' voice within me reaching out somewhere
> Toiling in the danger and in the morals of despair
>
> Don't have the inclination to look back on any mistake
> Like Cain, I now behold this chain of events that I must break
> In the fury of the moment I can see the Master's hand
> In every leaf that trembles, in every grain of sand
>
> Oh, the flowers of indulgence and the weeds of yesteryear
> Like criminals, they have choked the breath of conscience and good cheer

The sun beat down upon the steps of time to light the way
To ease the pain of idleness and the memory of decay

I gaze into the doorway of temptation's angry flame
And every time I pass that way I always hear my name
Then onward in my journey I come to understand
That every hair is numbered like every grain of sand"

There is a voice within him reaching out somewhere "toiling in the danger and in the morals of despair." He has come to know anguish. Now he doesn't want to look on any mistake. He is like Cain who must break the chain of events. He has come to see the Master's hand. He has come to know love and the fact he is accepted. He knows the truth of Jesus' words. He now leaves the indulgences "and the weeds of yesteryear". He knows the doorway of temptation's "angry flame". It still calls to him. But as he goes on in his journey he comes to understand "that every hair is numbered like every grain of sand."

"I have gone from rags to riches in the sorrow of the night
In the violence of a summer's dream, in the chill of a wintry
light
In the bitter dance of loneliness fading into space
In the broken mirror of innocence on each forgotten face

I hear the ancient footsteps like the motion of the sea
Sometimes I turn, there's someone there, other times it's
only me
I am hanging in the balance of the reality of man
Like every sparrow falling, like every grain of sand"

He looks over his life. He sees the "bitter dance of loneliness fading into space". He says he is "hanging in the balance of the reality of man, like every sparrow falling, like every grain of sand". Here he references Jesus' reference to how we are worth more than many sparrows. We are held in God's loving embrace, we are precious. We began with Daisy who felt invisible. When we begin to realise that we are precious in God's eyes we can look around us and see that others like Daisy are precious too. We are challenged to bring the love we experience to people like Daisy. We can pay attention in a new way to the world around us and the people we meet:

> "In the fury of the moment I can see the Master's hand
> In every leaf that trembles, in every grain of sand."

Printed in Great Britain
by Amazon

23998070R00059